PURSUIT OF TRUTH

PURSUIT OF
TRUTH

Revised Edition

W. V. QUINE

Harvard University Press
Cambridge, Massachusetts
London, England

TO

BURT DREBEN

firm friend and

constructive critic

down the decades

Seventh printing, 2003

Library of Congress Cataloging-in-Publication Data

Quine, W. V. (Willard Van Orman)
Pursuit of truth / W. V. Quine. — Rev. ed.
p.   cm.
Includes bibliographical references and index.
ISBN 0-674-73951-5 (pbk. : alk. paper)
1. Meaning (Philosophy)   2. Reference (Philosophy)   3. Knowledge,
Theory of.   4. Semantics (Philosophy)   I. Title.
B945.Q53P87   1992
121—dc20

92-5606
CIP

Preface to the Revised Edition

In May 1990, a mere four months after this book first appeared, I was in the gallant little Republic of San Marino for a week-long international colloquium on my philosophy. Six months later I was in medieval Girona, in Catalonia, giving the Josep Ferrater Mora Lectures—fifteen hours of them and five of discussion. Donald Davidson, Burton Dreben, Dagfinn Føllesdal, and Roger Gibson were all imported with me, to add depth and zest to the discussion. The busy months of preparation and the stimulating exchanges on these occasions sparked thoughts that would have made for a better book if the chronology had been inverted. I am approximating such an inversion as best I can by this early revised edition.

Old §13, "Ontological relativity," has become more emphatically "Ontology defused," and incorporates bits from my responses in the projected San Marino volume. My treatment of domestic meaning in §22 is utterly changed, and so also, thanks to Davidson's and Føllesdal's abetting, are §§28–29 on propositional attitudes.

March 1992   W.V.Q.

Preface to the First Edition

In these pages I have undertaken to update, sum up, and clarify my variously intersecting views on cognitive meaning, objective reference, and the grounds of knowledge. Some of the progress is expository and some substantive. The substance has been precipitating sporadically over the past ten years, and some of it has surfaced in lectures, informal discussions, and scattered paragraphs. In interrelating these thoughts I have occasionally found a faulty joint and have firmed it up to my satisfaction.

I intend this little book no less for my past readers than for my new ones, so I have curbed my exposition of things already belabored in my other books. I do retrace familiar ground where I see an improvement in the idea or its presentation, and also where the new reader needs a little briefing to be kept abreast.

The bits of the book that have previously appeared in print add up to a scant nine pages, and are identified on a back page. Unpublished lectures were a richer source. My lecture "The Mentalistic Heritage" in Calcutta, 1983, is a source of §31, and "The Forked Animal" yielded earlier parts of Chapter IV. That lecture was the third of four Immanuel Kant Lectures that I gave at Stanford in 1980. The title of the series of four was "Science and Sensibilia," a takeoff of John Austin's takeoff of Jane Austen. The four lectures appeared as a little book in Italian, *La scienza e i dati di senso,* translated by Michele Leonelli (Rome: Armando, 1987). Instead of publishing them intact in English, I have used portions of them in subsequent publications, as here.

Much of my lecture "Three Indeterminacies," presented at the Quine symposium at Washington University in April 1988, is woven into Chapter I, and bits into Chapter V. That lecture is to appear in the symposium volume, Barrett and Gibson, editors, *Perspectives on Quine* (Oxford: Blackwell). Another overlapping publication in the offing is "Truth," written at the request of the Institut International de Philosophie and slated for *Philosophical Problems Today* (The Hague: Nijhoff). I drew heavily on it for Chapter V, by prior arrangement.

I am blessed with bright and earnest readers. Leonelli wrote me from Pisa that my new blend of reification with observation gave him *una sorta di crampo mentale.* After two letters I began to feel the cramp myself. Result: a substantial revision of Chapters I and II. A letter from Felix Mühlhölzer in Munich prompted me to insert a couple of paragraphs recognizing the untidy side of scientific method. A difficulty spotted by Lars Bergström of Stockholm is now noted and dealt with in the text, and my indebtedness to Donald Davidson, Dagfinn Føllesdal, and Roger Gibson is noted at appropriate points. I am much indebted to Burton Dreben, who has read earlier drafts with care and insight and has made many helpful suggestions.

W.V.Q.

CONTENTS

PURSUIT OF TRUTH

σώζειν τὰ φαινόμενα.

PLATO

Save the surface and you save all.

SHERWIN-WILLIAMS

I

EVIDENCE

1. Stimulation and prediction

From impacts on our sensory surfaces, we in our collective and cumulative creativity down the generations have projected our systematic theory of the external world. Our system is proving successful in predicting subsequent sensory input. How have we done it?

Neurology is opening strange new vistas into what goes on between stimulation and perception. Psychology and more particularly psycholinguistics may be looked to for something to say about the passage from perception to expectation, generalization, and systematization. Evolutionary genetics throws further light on the latter matters, accounting for the standards of similarity that underlie our generalizations and hence our expectations. The heuristic of scientific creativity is illuminated also, anecdotally, by the history of science.

Within this baffling tangle of relations between our sensory stimulation and our scientific theory of the world, there is a segment that we can gratefully separate out and clarify without pursuing neurology, psychology, psycholinguistics, genetics, or history. It is the part where theory is tested by prediction. It is the relation of evidential support, and its essentials can be schematized by means of little more than logical analysis.

Not that prediction is the main purpose of science. One major purpose is understanding. Another is control and modification of the environment. Prediction can be a purpose too, but my present point is that it is the *test* of a theory, whatever the purpose.

It is common usage to say that the evidence for science is observation, and that what we predict are observations. But the notion of observation is awkward to analyze. Clarification has been sought by a shift to observable objects and events. But a gulf yawns between them and our immediate input from the external world, which is rather the triggering of our sensory receptors. I have cut through all this by settling for the triggering or stimulation itself and hence speaking, oddly perhaps, of the prediction of stimulation. By the stimulation undergone by a subject on a given occasion I just mean the temporally ordered set of all those of his exteroceptors that are triggered on that occasion.

Observation then drops out as a technical notion. So does evidence, if that was observation. We can deal with the question of evidence for science without help of 'evidence' as a technical term. We can make do instead with the notion of observation sentences.

2. *Observation sentences*

We were undertaking to examine the evidential support of science. That support, by whatever name, comes now to be seen as a relation of stimulation to scientific theory. Theory consists of sentences, or is couched in them; and logic connects sentences to sentences. What we need, then, as initial links in those connecting chains, are some sentences that are directly and firmly associated with our stimulations. Each should be associated affirmatively with some range of one's stimulations and negatively with some range. The sentence should command the subject's assent or dissent outright, on the occasion of a stimulation in the appropriate range, without further investigation and independently of what he may have been engaged in at the time. A further requirement is intersubjectivity: unlike a report of a feeling, the sentence must command the same verdict from all linguistically competent witnesses of the occasion.

I call them *observation sentences*. Examples are 'It's raining', 'It's getting cold', 'That's a rabbit'. Unlike 'Men are mortal', they are *occasion* sentences: true on some occasions, false on others. Sometimes it is raining, sometimes not. Briefly stated, then, an observation sentence is an occasion sentence on which speakers of the language can agree outright on witnessing the occasion. See further §15.

Observationality is vague at the edges. There are gradations in an individual's readiness to assent. What had passed for an observation sentence, say 'That's a swan', may to the subject's own surprise leave him undecided when he encounters a black specimen. He may have to resort to convention to settle his usage. We shall need now and again to remind ourselves thus of the untidiness of human behavior, but meanwhile we foster perspicuity by fancying boundaries.

The range of stimulations associated with an observation sentence, affirmatively or negatively, I call its affirmative or negative *stimulus meaning* for the given speaker. Each of the stimulations, by my definition, is global; it is the set of *all* the triggered exteroceptors, not just the ones that happened to elicit behavior. Hence the stimulations encompassed in a stimulus meaning will differ wildly from one another in their ineffective firings, but in their effective core they are bound to be similar to one another in some respect, by the subject's lights;[1] similar, that is, in eliciting similar behavior. His according them all the same observation sentence is itself a case of similar elicited behavior.

An observation sentence may consist of a single noun or adjective, thought of as a sentence; thus 'Rain', 'Cold', or 'Rabbit', for 'It's raining', 'It's cold', 'It's a rabbit'. Observation sentences also may be compounded to form further observation sentences, for example by simple *conjunction*: 'The sun is rising and birds are singing'. Another way of compounding them is *predication:* 'This pebble is blue', as a compound of 'Lo, a pebble' and 'Lo, blue'. An equivalent rendering is simply 'Blue pebble'; they have the same stimulus meaning. But they are not equivalent to the mere conjunction 'Lo, a pebble, and lo, blue'. Their connection is tighter. The conjunction is fulfilled so long as the stimulation shows each of the component observation sentences to be fulfilled somewhere in the scene—thus a white pebble here, a blue flower over there. On the other hand the predication focuses the two fulfillments, requiring them to coincide or amply overlap. The blue must encompass the pebble. It may also extend beyond; the construction is not symmetric.

What brought us to an examination of observation sentences was our quest of the link between observation and theory. The observation sentence is the means of verbalizing the prediction that checks a theory. The requirement

[1]Hence perceptually similar, not receptually. *Roots of Reference,* pp. 16–18.

that it command a verdict outright is what makes it a final checkpoint. The requirement of intersubjectivity is what makes science objective.

Observation sentences are thus the vehicle of scientific evidence, we might say—though without venturing a definition of 'evidence' itself. But also they are the entering wedge in the learning of language. The infant's first acquisitions in cognitive language are rudimentary observation sentences, including 'Mama', 'Milk', and the like as one-word observation sentences. They become associated with stimulations by the conditioning of responses. Their direct association with concurrent stimulation is essential if the child is to acquire them without prior language, and the requirement of intersubjectivity is essential in order that he learn the expressions from other speakers on appropriately shared occasions.

That observation sentences serve in both ways—as vehicles of scientific evidence and as entering wedge into language—is no cause for wonder. Observation sentences are the link between language, scientific or not, and the real world that language is all about.

Observation sentences as I have defined them far exceed the primitive ones that are the child's entering wedge. Many of them are learned not by simple conditioning or imitation, but by subsequent construction from sophisticated vocabulary. The requirement of direct correspondence to ranges of stimulation can be met either way. Which ones are learned directly by conditioning, and which ones indirectly through higher language, will vary from person to person. But the two requirements, intersubjectivity and correspondence to stimulation, assure us that any observation sentence *could* be learned in the direct way. We hear our fellow speakers affirming and denying the sentence on just the occasions when we are stimulated in the characteristic ways, and we join in.

3. Theory-laden?

My definition of observation sentence is of my devising, but the term is not. Philosophers have long treated in their several ways of what they called observation terms or observation sentences. But it has now become fashionable to question the notions, and to claim that the purportedly observable is theory-laden in varying degrees. It is pointed out that when scientists marshal and check their own data or one another's, they press no farther than is needed to assure agreement among witnesses conversant with the subject; for they are reasonable men. 'The mixture is at 180°C' and 'Hydrogen sulfide is escaping' are observational enough for any of them, and more recondite reports are observational enough for some. I agree that the practical notion of observation is thus relative to one or another limited community, rather than to the whole speech community. An observation sentence for a community is an occasion sentence on which members of the community can agree outright on witnessing the occasion.

For philosophical purposes we can probe deeper, however, and reach a single standard for the whole speech community. Observable in this sense is whatever would be attested to on the spot by any witness in command of the language and his five senses. If scientists were perversely to persist in demanding further evidence beyond what sufficed for agreement, their observables would reduce for the most part to those of the whole speech community. Just a few, such as the indescribable smell of some uncommon gas, would resist reduction.

But what has all this to do with a sentence's being theory-laden or theory-free? My definition distinguishes observation sentences from others, whether relative to special communities or to the general one, without reference to theory-freedom. There is a sense, as we shall now see, in which they are all theory-laden, even the most primitive ones, and there is a sense in which none are, even the most professional ones.

Think first of primitive ones, the entering wedge in language learning. They are associated as wholes to appropriate ranges of stimulation, by conditioning. Component words are there merely as component syllables, theory-free. But these words recur in theoretical contexts in the fullness of time. It is precisely this sharing of words, by observation sentences and theoretical sentences, that provides logical connections between the two kinds of sentences and makes observation relevant to scientific theory. Retrospectively those once innocent observation sentences are theory-laden indeed. An observation sentence containing no word more technical than 'water' will join forces with theoretical sentences containing terms as technical as 'H_2O'. Seen holophrastically, as conditioned to stimulatory situations, the sentence is theory-free; seen analytically, word by word, it is theory-laden. Insofar as observation sentences bear on science at all, affording evidence and tests, there has to be this retrospective theory-lading along with the pristine holophrastic freedom from theory. To impugn their observationality thus retrospectively is to commit what Firth (p. 100) called the fallacy of conceptual retrojection.

More sophisticated observation sentences, including those of specialized scientific communities, are similarly two-faced, even though learned by composition rather than direct conditioning. What qualifies them as observation sentences is still their holophrastic association with fixed ranges of sensory stimulation, however that association be acquired. Holophrastically they function still as theory-free, like C. I. Lewis's "expressive" sentences (p. 179), though when taken retrospectively word by word the self-same sentences are theory-laden, like his "objective" ones.

When epistemology rounded the linguistic turn, talk of observable objects gave way to talk of observation terms. It was a good move, but not good enough. Observation sentences were distinguished from theoretical ones only derivatively, as containing observation terms to the exclusion of theory-laden or theoretical terms. Consequently Reichenbach and others felt a need for "bridge principles" to relate the two kinds of sentences. No bridge is wanted, we now see, and bridging is the wrong figure. Starting with sentences as we have done rather than with terms, we see no bar to a sharing of vocabulary by the two kinds of sentences; and it is the shared vocabulary that links them.

Starting with sentences has conferred the further boon of freeing the definition of observation sentence from any dependence on the distinction between the theory-free and the theory-laden. Yet a third advantage of this move is that we can then study the acquisition and use of observation sentences without prejudging what objects, if any, the component words are meant to refer to. We thus are freed to speculate on the nature of reification and its utility for scientific theory—a topic for Chapter II. Taking terms as starting point would have meant finessing reification and conceding objective reference out of hand, without considering what it is for or what goes into it.

4. *Observation categoricals*

The support of a theory by observation stands forth most explicitly in experiment, so let us look into that. The scientist has a backlog of accepted theory, and is considering a hypothesis for possible incorporation into it. The theory tells him that if the hypothesis under consideration is true, then, whenever a certain observable situation is set up, a certain effect should be observed. So he sets up the situation in question. If the predicted effect fails to appear, he abandons his hypothesis. If the effect does appear, his hypothesis may be true and so can be tentatively added to his backlog of theory.

Thus suppose a team of field mineralogists have turned up an unfamiliar crystalline mineral of a distinctively pinkish cast. They speak of it provisionally as *litholite,* for want of a better name. One of them conjectures its chemical composition. This is the hypothesis, of which I shall spare myself the details. From his backlog of chemical lore he reasons that if this chemical hypothesis is true, then any piece of litholite should emit hydrogen sulfide when heated above 180°C. These last provisions are the observables; for our mineralogist and his colleagues know litholite when they see it and hydrogen sulfide when they smell it, and they can read a thermometer.

The test of a hypothesis thus hinges on a logical relation of implication. On one side, the theoretical, we have the backlog of accepted theory plus the hypothesis. This combination does the implying. On the other side, the observational, we have an implied generality that the experimenter can directly test, directly challenge—in this case by heating some of the pink stuff and sniffing.

A generality that is compounded of observables in this way—'Whenever this, that'—is what I call an *observation categorical*. It is compounded of observation sentences. The 'Whenever' is not intended to reify times and quantify over them. What is intended is an irreducible generality prior to any objective reference. It is a generality to the effect that the circumstances described in the one observation sentence are invariably accompanied by those described in the other.[2]

Though compounded of two occasion sentences, the observation categorical is itself a *standing* sentence, and hence fair game for implication by scientific theory. It thus solves the problem of linking theory logically to observation, as well as epitomizing the experimental situation.

That situation is where a hypothesis is being tested by an experiment. An opposite situation is equally familiar: a chance observation may prompt us to conjecture a new observation categorical, and we may invent a theoretical hypothesis to explain it. For example, we might notice willows leaning over a stream. This suggests the observation categorical:

(1)   When a willow grows at the water's edge, it leans over the water.

[2] The observation categorical is not to be confused with the observation *conditional*, a less fruitful notion that I ventured in 1975. The observation conditional is formed from two standing sentences each of which has been built upon an observation sentence with help of theory. See *Theories and Things*, pp. 26–27.

This suggests, in turn, a theoretical hypothesis: 'A willow root nourishes mainly its own side of the tree'. Taken together with prior bits of theory, such as that roots get more nourishment from wetter ground, and that nourishment promotes the growth of branches, the hypothesis is found to imply the observation categorical. Other observation categoricals will be implied too, and the continued testing of the hypothesis would proceed by testing various of them, along with further testing of the one that happened to suggest the hypothesis.

The observation categorical (1) exceeds my definition in a subtle way: it is not compounded of two self-sufficient observation sentences. It cannot be read 'When a willow grows at the water's edge, *a willow* leans over the water'. The component observation sentences have to bear not just on the same scene, this time, but on the same part of the scene, the same willow. Such was the force of 'it' in (1). We have what may be called a *focal* observation categorical, as distinct from a *free* one.

In §2 we saw a contrast between conjunction and predication. Now the free observation categorical generalizes merely on a conjunction, and claims that every occasion presenting the one feature will present the other somewhere about. The focal observation categorical generalizes rather on a predicational observation sentence. (1) generalizes on the predication 'This riverine willow leans over the water' to say that they all do.

A more succinct predicational observation sentence is 'This raven is black', or 'Black raven'. It generalizes to the focal observation categorical 'Whenever there is a raven, *it* is black', or, succinctly, 'All ravens are black'.

5. *Test and refutation*

An observation categorical is tested by pairs of observations. It is not conclusively verified by observations that are conformable to it, but it is refuted by a pair of observations, one affirmative and one negative—thus observation of litholite at 180°C but absence of hydrogen sulfide, or observation of riverine willows leaning away from the water. The free observation categorical 'When the sun comes up the birds sing' is refuted by observing sunrise among silent birds.

The observational test of scientific hypotheses, in turn, and indeed of sentences generally, consists in testing observation categoricals that they imply. Here again, as in the case of the observation categorical itself, there is no conclusive verification, but only refutation. Refute an observation categorical, by an affirmative and a negative observation, and you have refuted whatever implied it.

Traditional epistemology sought grounds in sensory experience capable of implying our theories about the world, or at least of endowing those theories with some increment of probability. Sir Karl Popper has long stressed, to the contrary, that observation serves only to refute theory and not to support it. We have now been seeing in a schematic way why this is so.

But again we must bear in mind, as in §2, that we are schematizing: positing sharp boundaries where none can be drawn. The pair of observations in purported refutation of an observation categorical may be indecisive because of unforeseen indecision over the stimulus meaning of one of the pair of observation sentences, as in the case of the black swan or an albino raven. A theory that implied the observation categorical 'All swans are white', or 'All ravens are black', might or might not be refuted by the discovery of the odd specimen, depending on our own decision regarding the vague stimulus meaning of the word. In both examples the verbal usages actually adopted, which do admit black swans and blond ravens, are the ones that make for the smoother terminology in the overall theory.

It is clearly true, moreover, that one continually reasons not only in refutation of hypotheses but in support of them. This, however, is a matter of arguing logically or probabilistically from other beliefs already held. It is where the technology of probability and mathematical statistics is brought to bear. Some of those supporting beliefs may be observational, but they contribute support only in company with others that are theoretical. Pure observation lends only negative evidence, by refuting an observation categorical that a proposed theory implies.

6. Holism

Let us recall that the hypothesis regarding the chemical composition of litholite did not imply its observation categorical single-handed. It implied it with the help of a backlog of accepted scientific theory. In order to deduce an observation categorical from a given hypothesis, we may have to enlist the aid of other theoretical sentences and of many common-sense platitudes that go without saying, and perhaps the aid even of arithmetic and other parts of mathematics.

In that situation, the falsity of the observation categorical does not conclusively refute the hypothesis. What it refutes is the conjunction of sentences that was needed to imply the observation categorical. In order to retract that conjunction we do not have to retract the hypothesis in question; we could retract some other sentence of the conjunction instead. This is the important insight called *holism*. Pierre Duhem made much of it early in this century, but not too much.

The scientist thinks of his experiment as a test specifically of his new hypothesis, but only because this was the sentence he was wondering about and is prepared to reject. Moreover, there are also the situations where he has no preconceived hypothesis, but just happens upon an anomalous phenomenon. It is a case of his happening upon a counter-instance of an observation categorical which, according to his current theory as a whole, ought to have been true. So he looks to his theory with a critical eye.

Over-logicizing, we may picture the accommodation of a failed observation categorical as follows. We have before us some set S of purported truths that was found jointly to imply the false categorical. Implication may be taken here simply as deducibility by the logic of truth functions, quantification, and identity. (We can always provide for more substantial consequences by incorporating appropriate premises explicitly into S.) Now some one or more of the sentences in S are going to have to be rescinded. We exempt some members of S from this threat on determining that the fateful implication still holds without their help. Any purely logical truth is thus exempted, since it adds nothing to what S would logically imply anyway; and sundry irrelevant sentences in S will be exempted as well. Of the remaining members of S, we rescind one that seems most suspect, or least crucial to our overall theory. We heed a maxim of minimum mutilation. If the remaining members of S still conspire to imply the false categorical, we try rescinding another and restoring the first. If the false categorical is still implied, we try rescinding both. We continue thus until the implication is defused.

But this is only the beginning. We must also track down sets of sentences elsewhere, in our overall theory, that imply these newly rescinded beliefs; for those must be defused too. We continue thus until consistency seems to be restored. Such is the mutilation that the maxim of minimum mutilation is meant to minimize.

In particular the maxim constrains us, in our choice of what sentences of S to rescind, to safeguard any purely mathematical truth; for mathematics infiltrates all branches of our system of the world, and its disruption would reverberate intolerably. If asked why he spares mathematics, the scientist will perhaps say that its laws are necessarily true; but I think we have here an explanation, rather, of mathematical necessity itself. It resides in our unstated policy of shielding mathematics by exercising our freedom to reject other beliefs instead.

So the choice of which of the beliefs to reject is indifferent only so far as the failed observation categorical is concerned, and not on other counts. It is well, we saw, not to rock the boat more than need be. Simplicity of the resulting theory is another guiding consideration, however, and if the scientist sees his way to a big gain in simplicity he is even prepared to rock the boat very considerably for the sake of it. But the ultimate objective is so to choose the revision as to maximize future success in prediction: future coverage of true observation categoricals. There is no recipe for this, but maximization of simplicity and minimization of mutilation are maxims by which science strives for vindication in future predictions.

It is difficult to see how anyone can question holism, in the sense now before us. Grünbaum has indeed argued against holism, but in a stronger sense than is here entertained. He construes holism as claiming that when a prediction fails, we can always save the threatened hypothesis by so revising the backlog of accepted theory that it, plus the threatened hypothesis, will imply the *failure* of the prediction. I am making no such presumption. Inactivating the false implication is all that is at stake. Explaining the unexpected counter-observation is quite another step of scientific progress, which may or may not be made in the fullness of time.

Holism in this moderate sense is an obvious but vital correction of the naive conception of scientific sentences as endowed each with its own separable empirical content. Content is shared, even by mathematics insofar as it gets applied.

7. Empirical content

Stimulus meanings have fuzzy boundaries, as witness again the black swan and the albino raven. If we imagine sharp demarcation, however, we can build up to a deceptively precise but withal instructive definition of empirical content.

Call an observation categorical *analytic* for a given speaker if, as in 'Robins are birds', the affirmative stimulus meaning for him of the one component is included in that of the other. Otherwise *synthetic*. Call a sentence or set of sentences *testable* if it implies some synthetic observation categoricals. Call two observation categoricals *synonymous* if their respective components have the same stimulus meanings. Then the *empirical content* of a testable sentence or set of sentences for that speaker is the set of all the synthetic observation categoricals that it implies, plus all synonymous ones. I add the synonymous ones so that merely verbal variation will not obstruct sameness of content.

Having thus defined empirical content and hence empirical equivalence for the individual speaker, we can call two sentences or sets of sentences equivalent for a whole community when equivalent for each member.

Some unconjoined single sentences qualify as testable, notably the synthetic observation categoricals themselves. For the most part, however, a testable set or conjunction of sentences has to be pretty big, and such is the burden of holism. It is a question of critical semantic mass.

We must recognize, along with the idealization of stimulus meanings, a significant degree of idealization in the foregoing account of hypothesis-testing. The scientist does not tabulate in advance the whole fund of theoretical tenets and technical assumptions, much less the commonsense platitudes and mathematical laws, that are needed in addition to his currently targeted hypothesis in order to imply the observation categorical of his experiment. It would be a Herculean labor, not to say Augean, to sort out all the premisses and logical strands of implication that ultimately link theory with observation, if or insofar as linked they be.

Worse, it seems that in many cases no such marshaling of tacit premisses could quite clinch the observation categorical, because of vagueness. The situation is illustrated by the near-platitude

(1)   Sodium chloride dissolves in water.

Notoriously, this is tenable only *ceteris paribus,* and the *cetera* are left vague. Normally one just treats (1) as true and admits it to the backlog of auxiliary tenets, implicitly or explicitly. If an experimenter faced with a negative result elects to save his hypothesis by tampering with the auxiliary tenets, and with (1) in particular, he will do so by developing a subsidiary theory to account for an exception to (1). In general (1) is accepted as a vague statement of strong probability, open to question only where the improbable counter-instance can be plausibly accounted for.

Similar cushioning shields much of science, it would seem, from the simple probe of observation categoricals. It has even been argued that our broadest scientific laws escape evidence altogether. Yosida writes (pp. 207–208) that they "may become out of fashion, . . . they are never refuted by direct observation, they are the old soldiers who never die but only fade away."

The point of the doctrine of observation categoricals, meanwhile, is to explain the bearing of sensory stimulation upon scientific theory so long and insofar as science has not parted its empirical moorings. My concern has been with the central logical structure of empirical evidence. In fused phrases of Kant and Russell, it is a question of how our knowledge of the external world is possible. Science does stay responsive somehow to sensory stimulation both early and late, but its mode of response after the parting of the moorings eludes my schematism. My definition of empirical content, accordingly, applies only to sentences and sets of sentences that are *testable* in the defined sense of flatly implying synthetic observation categoricals.

8. Norms and aims

I am of that large minority or small majority who repudiate the Cartesian dream of a foundation for scientific certainty firmer than scientific method itself. But I remain occupied, we see, with what has been central to traditional epistemology, namely the relation of science to its sensory data. I approach it as an input–output relation within flesh-and-blood denizens of an antecedently acknowledged external world, a relation open to inquiry as a chapter of the science of that world. To emphasize my dissociation from the Cartesian dream, I have written of neural receptors and their stimulation rather than of sense or sensibilia. I call the pursuit naturalized epistemology, but I have no quarrel with traditionalists who protest my retention of the latter word. I agree with them that repudiation of the Cartesian dream is no minor deviation.

But they are wrong in protesting that the normative element, so characteristic of epistemology, goes by the board. Insofar as theoretical epistemology gets naturalized into a chapter of theoretical science, so normative epistemology gets naturalized into a chapter of engineering: the technology of anticipating sensory stimulation.

The most notable norm of naturalized epistemology actually coincides with that of traditional epistemology. It is simply the watchword of empiricism: *nihil in mente quod non prius in sensu*. This is a prime specimen of naturalized epistemology, for it is a finding of natural science itself, however fallible, that our information about the world comes only through impacts on our sensory receptors. And still the point is normative, warning us against telepaths and soothsayers.

Moreover, naturalized epistemology on its normative side is occupied with heuristics generally—with the whole strategy of rational conjecture in the framing of scientific hypotheses. In the present pages I have been treating rather of the testing of a theory after it has been thought up, this being where the truth conditions and empirical content lie; so I have passed over the thinking up, which is where the normative considerations come in. Ullian and I did go into it somewhat in *The Web of Belief,* listing five virtues to seek in a hypothesis: conservatism, generality, simplicity, refutability, and modesty. Further counsel is available anecdotally in the history of hard science. In a more technical vein, normative naturalized epistemology tangles with margin of error, random deviation, and whatever else goes into the applied mathematics of statistics. (See §5.)

But when I cite predictions as the checkpoints of science, I do not see that as normative. I see it as defining a particular language game, in Wittgenstein's phrase: the game of science, in contrast to other good language games such as fiction and poetry. A sentence's claim to scientific status rests on what it contributes to a theory whose checkpoints are in prediction.

I stressed in §1 that prediction is not the main purpose of the science game. It is what decides the game, like runs and outs in baseball. It is occasionally the purpose, and in primitive times it gave primitive science its survival value. But nowadays the overwhelming purposes of the science game are technology and understanding.

The science game is not committed to the physical, whatever that means. Bodies have long since diffused into swarms of particles, and the Bose-Einstein statistic (§13) has challenged the particularity of the particle. Even telepathy and clairvoyance are scientific options, however moribund. It would take some extraordinary evidence to enliven them, but, if that were to happen, then empiricism itself—the crowning norm, we saw, of naturalized epistemology—would go by the board. For remember that that norm, and naturalized epistemology itself, are integral to science, and science is fallible and corrigible.

Science after such a convulsion would still be science, the same old language game, hinging still on checkpoints in sensory prediction. The collapse of empiricism would admit extra input by telepathy or revelation, but the test of the resulting science would still be predicted sensation.

In that extremity it might indeed be well to modify the game itself, and take on as further checkpoints the predicting of telepathic and divine input as well as of sensory input. It is idle to bulwark definitions against implausible contingencies.

II

REFERENCE

9. Bodies

There were advantages, we saw (§3), in starting with observation sentences rather than terms. One advantage was that the nature and utility of reification could be deferred for consideration until an epistemological setting had been sketched in. We are now at that stage.

Incipient reification can already be sensed in the predicational observation sentences (§2). That mode of combination favors, as components, observation sentences that focus on conspicuously limited portions of the scene; for the compound expresses coincidence of such foci.

A second step of reification, and a step beyond ordinary observation sentences, was recognizable in the move to focal observation categoricals (§4). I think of the child as first mastering this construction, like the free observation categorical, simply as a generalized expression of expectation: whenever this, that. For her the difference between the two kinds of categorical would not at first obtrude. The difference is, we recall, that the focal categorical requires the two features—'Raven' and 'Black', say—to fuse in the scene, while the free categorical does not. However, the scenes first associated with 'Raven' will show a raven at the salient focus, and those first associated with 'Black' will show black at the salient focus. Insofar, the free categorical already meets the focal demand. The difference between the free and the focal in other cases, and between conjunction and predication (§2), can gradually dawn on the child in its own time.

By virtue of its narrowed focus, however, the focal observation categorical—unlike the free one—has decidedly the air of general discourse about bodies: willows in the one example, ravens in the other. This is where I see bodies materializing, ontologically speaking: as ideal nodes at the foci of intersecting observation sentences. Here, I suggest, is the root of reification.

For the very young child, who has not got beyond observation sentences, the recurrent presentation of a body is much on a par with similarities of stimulation that clearly do not prompt reification. Recurrent confrontation of a ball is on a par at first with mere recurrent exposure to sunshine or cool air: the question whether it is the same old ball or one like it makes no more sense than whether it is the same old sunbeam, the same old breeze. Experience is in its *feature-placing* stage, in Strawson's phrase. Individuation comes only later.

True, an infant is observed to expect a steadily moving object to reappear after it passes behind a screen; but this all happens within the specious present, and reflects rather the expectation of continuity of a present feature than the reification of an intermittently absent object. Again a dog's recognition of a recurrent individual is beside the point; the dog is responding to a distinctive odor or other trait, unavailable in the case of qualitatively indistinguishable balls.

To us the question whether we are seeing the same old ball or just a similar one is meaningful even in cases where it remains unanswered. It is here that the reification of bodies is full blown. Our venerable theory of the persistence and recurrence of bodies is characteristic of the use of reification in integrating our system of the world. If I were to try to decide whether the penny now in my pocket is the one that was there last week, or just another one like it, I would have to explore quite varied aspects of my overall scheme of things, so as to reconstruct the simplest, most plausible account of my interim movements, costumes, and expenditures.

Perhaps such indirect equating and distinguishing of bodies is achieved by some other animals to some extent. Perhaps a dog seeking a ball that disappeared fairly recently in one quarter will not settle for a similar ball at an unlikely distance. However that may be, it seems clear that such reification of bodies across time is beyond the reach of observation sentences and categoricals. Substantial reification is theoretical.

10. *Values of variables*

Even our sophisticated conception of enduring and recurrent bodies, so characteristic of our human ontology, is for us little more than a beginning. With our progressive systematization of science we have gone on to reify liquids and the invisible air, and we have integrated these things with bodies by reckoning them as aggregates of bodies too small to be detected. Nor have we stopped here. Abstract objects have long since proved indispensable to natural science—thus numbers, functions, classes.

At this level a question arises of what to count as reification, and what to count rather as just a useful but

ontologically noncommittal turn of phrase; for the idea that
seemed to mark so decisively the reification of bodies,
namely persistence between exposures, makes no sense for
abstract objects. I have urged elsewhere that the most decisive general marks of reification in our language and kindred ones are the pronouns, and indeed it was 'it' in (1) of §4
that signaled those early rumblings of reification in the focal
observation categoricals. The theme is taken up in full by
the relative pronouns and their auxiliaries.[1] When a language is regimented in the logical notation of the predicate
calculus, the role of such pronouns is played by bound variables.

Observation sentences are to be taken holophrastically
from the standpoint of evidence, I urged (§3), and analytically word by word from the retrospective standpoint of
theory. From the latter standpoint a focal observation
categorical is an outright quantification. 'Ravens are black'
becomes

$$\forall x(x \text{ is a raven} \cdot \rightarrow \cdot x \text{ is black}).$$

Free observational categoricals would be construed similarly, usually by quantifying over times or places.

So I have insisted down the years that to be is to be the
value of a variable. More precisely, what one takes there to
be are what one admits as values of one's bound variables.
The point has been recognized as obvious and trivial, but it
has also been deemed unacceptable, even by readers who
share my general philosophical outlook. Let me sort out
some of the considerations.

The artificial notation '$\exists x$' of existential quantification is
explained merely as a symbolic rendering of the words

[1] See *Theories and Things*, pp. 5–6.

'there is something x such that'. So, whatever more one may care to say about being or existence, what there are taken to be are assuredly just what are taken to qualify as values of 'x' in quantifications. The point is thus trivial and obvious.

It has been objected that what there is is a question of fact and not of language. True enough. Saying or implying what there is, however, is a matter of language; and this is the place of the bound variables.

It has been objected that the logical notation of quantification is an arbitrary and parochial standard to adopt for ontological commitment. The answer is that the standard is transferable to any alternative language, insofar as we are agreed on how to translate quantification into it. For predicate-functor logic, thus, the equivalent principle is that what one takes there to be are what one takes one's monadic predicates (complements included) to be true of. For ordinary English what one takes there to be are what one takes one's relative pronouns to refer to. Ordinary discourse is indeed seldom meticulous about ontology, and consequently an assessment based on the relative pronouns of ordinary discourse is apt to bespeak a pretty untidy world; but ontological clarity and economy can be promoted by paraphrase, if one so desires, in terms still of relative clauses and pronouns rather than quantifiers and bound variables. The notation of quantification is what is most usual and familiar, currently, where one is expressly concerned with ontological niceties; hence my choice of it as paradigm.

One thinks of reference, first and foremost, as relating names and other singular terms to their objects. Yet singular terms often fail to refer to anything. Conversely, also, set theory teaches that there are bound to be individually unspecifiable objects—unspecifiable irrational numbers, notably—no matter how rich our notation and cumbersome our expressions. Variables, on the other hand, take all objects as values, irrespective of specifiability.

Once our language is regimented to fit the predicate calculus, moreover, it is easy and instructive to dispense with singular terms altogether, leaving variables as the only link to objects. The underlying principle here is the equivalence of '$\exists x(Fx$ and $a = x)$' to 'Fa'; for this enables us to maneuver every occurrence of 'a' into the context '$a =$ ', and then to treat that context as an indissoluble predicate 'A', absorbing the singular term. Singular terms can still be recovered afterward as a convenient shorthand, by introducing singular description in Russell's way and defining 'a' as '$(\imath x)Ax$'.[2]

If in some language we are at a loss to arrive at a satisfactory contextual translation of 'there is', and hence of existential quantification, then we are at a loss to assess the ontology of the speakers of that language. Some languages are perhaps so unlike ours that any translation of 'there is' or '$\exists x$', however cunningly contextual, would be too farfetched and Procrustean to rest with. To entertain the notion of an ontology at all, known or unknown, for the speakers of such a language would be an unwarranted projection on our part of a parochial category appropriate only to our own linguistic circle. Thus I do recognize that the question of ontological commitment is parochial, though within a much broader parish than that of the speakers and writers of symbolic logic.

[2] See *Word and Object*, pp. 176–190.

11. *Utility of reification*

We detected the first hint of reification in the predicational compounding of observation sentences, as contrasted with simple conjunction. Predication is a stronger connection than conjunction; it requires immersion of the pebble in the blue (§2) and the raven in the black, while mere conjunction allows the features to go their separate ways.

At its inception, thus, we find reification contributing to the logical connections between observation and theory by tightening up on truth functions. Elsewhere I have made the point more emphatically by a four-part example:

(1)   A white cat is facing a dog and bristling.

Four simple observation sentences underlie this. One is 'Cat', or, on the analogy of the ontologically innocent 'It's raining', 'It's catting'. The others are 'White', 'Dog-facing', and 'Bristling'. But (1) cannot be rendered as a mere conjunction of these four, because the conjunction is too loose. It tells us only that the four things are going on in the same scene. We want them all in the same part of the scene, superimposed. It is this tightening that is achieved by subjecting the four-fold conjunction to existential quantification, thus:

> Something is catting and is white and is
> dog-facing and is bristling,

which is to say (1). An object has been posited, a cat.[3]

For all its complexity, (1) is an observation sentence. It *could* be acquired by direct conditioning to the complex

---

[3] My approach here was inspired by Davidson's logic of adverbs, in his *Essays on Action and Events,* pp. 166. See my "Events and Reification."

situation that it reports, if this situation were to recur and be reported oftener than one is prepared to expect. But it is illustrative of an unlimited lot of equally complex and unlikely observation sentences. There is no hope of direct acquisition of each; systematic construction from elements is mandatory. Reification, we see, to the rescue.

For purposes of that context, a cat of the moment would suffice; no need of an enduring cat. To illustrate the need of an enduring cat I must go beyond observation sentences and suppose that we have somehow worked our way far enough up into scientific theory to treat of time; earlier and later. Suppose then we want to convey this thought:

(2)   If a cat eats a spoiled fish and sickens, then she will thereafter avoid fish.

We cannot treat this as a simple "if-then" compound of two self-sufficient component sentences. Like the "and" of the preceding example, the "if-then" connection is too weak. It has to be the same cat in both sentences, and hence an enduring cat. Our sentence is really a universally quantified conditional:

> Everything is such that if it is a cat and it eats a spoiled fish and it sickens then it will thereafter avoid fish.

Hilary Putnam and Charles Parsons have both remarked on ways of economizing on abstract objects by recourse to a modal operator of possibility.[4] We have just observed the other side of the same coin: the positing of objects can serve to reinforce the weak truth functions without recourse to modal operators. Where there are such trade-offs to choose

---

[4]Putnam, pp. 47–49; Parsons, pp. 44–47.

between, I am for positing the objects. I posit abstract ones grudgingly on the whole, but gratefully where the alternative course would call for modal operators. (Cf. §30.)

My examples offer a crude notion of how it may be that reification and reference contribute to the elaborate structure that relates science to its sensory evidence. At its most rudimentary level, reification is a device for focusing observation sentences convergently; thus (1). Anaphora, clinching of cross-reference, continues to be its business also at more sophisticated levels, as in (2). It is no coincidence that this is precisely the business also of pronouns, or bound variables. To be is to be the value of a variable.

12. Indifference of ontology

Reference and ontology recede thus to the status of mere auxiliaries. True sentences, observational and theoretical, are the alpha and omega of the scientific enterprise. They are related by structure, and objects figure as mere nodes of the structure. What particular objects there may be is indifferent to the truth of observation sentences, indifferent to the support they lend to the theoretical sentences, indifferent to the success of the theory in its predictions.

The point can be accentuated by invoking what I have called *proxy functions*. A proxy function is any explicit one-to-one transformation, f, defined over the objects in our purported universe. By 'explicit' I mean that for any object x, specified in an acceptable notation, we can specify fx. Suppose now we shift our ontology by reinterpreting each of our predicates as true rather of the correlates fx of the objects x that it had been true of. Thus, where 'Px' originally meant that x was a P, we reinterpret 'Px' as meaning that x is f of a P. Correspondingly for two-place predicates and higher. Singular terms can be passed over in view of §10. We leave all the sentences as they were, letter for letter, merely reinterpreting. The observation sentences remain associated with the same sensory stimulations as before, and the logical interconnections remain intact. Yet the objects of the theory have been supplanted as drastically as you please.[5]

Sometimes we can waive the requirement that the proxy function be one to one. Thus consider Gödel's numbering of expressions, in the course of his proof of his famous incompleteness theorem. In one's global theory of things it would be unnatural to say that the expressions are identical with those numbers, but still there might be no call to distinguish them. In that event a proxy function might just as well treat them alike, assigning the same proxies to the expressions as to the numbers.

However, one-to-one proxy functions were all I needed for my present purpose, namely, to show the indifference of ontology. A more radical case for the indifference of ontology is afforded by the Löwenheim-Skolem theorem, in a strengthened form due to Hilbert and Bernays.[6] When applied to a theory that has been fitted to predicate logic, cleared of singular terms, and encompassed in a finite lot of axioms, this theorem enables us to express a truth-preserving reinterpretation of the predicates that makes the universe come to consist merely of natural numbers 0, 1, 2, ... This theorem does not, like proxy functions, carry each of the old objects into a definite new one, a particular number. This was not to be hoped for, since some infinite do-

---

[5] For more see *Ontological Relativity*, pp. 55–58.
[6] See *Methods of Logic*, 4th ed., pp. 209–211.

mains—notably that of the irrational numbers—are of too high a cardinality to be exhausted by correlation with natural numbers. Despite this limitation, however, the reinterpretations leave all observation sentences associated with the same old stimulations and all logical links undisturbed.

Once we have appropriately regimented our system of the world or part of it, we can so reinterpret it as to get by with only the slender ontology of the whole numbers; such is the strengthened Löwenheim-Skolem theorem. But we could not have arrived at our science in the first place under that interpretation, since the numbers do not correspond one by one to the reifications that were our stepping stones. Practically, heuristically, we must presumably pursue science in the old way or within the reach, at least, of proxy functions.

13. Ontology defused

We found that two ontologies, if explicitly correlated one to one, are empirically on a par; there is no empirical ground for choosing the one rather than the other. What is empirically significant in an ontology is just its contribution of neutral nodes to the structure of the theory. We could reinterpret 'Tabitha' as designating no longer the cat, but the whole cosmos minus the cat; or, again, as designating the cat's singleton, or unit class. Reinterpreting the rest of our terms for bodies in corresponding fashion, we come out with an ontology interchangeable with our familiar one. As wholes they are empirically indistinguishable. Bodies still continue, under each interpretation, to be distinct from their cosmic complements and from their singletons; they are distinguished in a relativistic way, by their roles relative to one another and to the rest of the ontology. Hence my watchword *ontological relativity*. But see further §20.

The importance of the distinction between term and observation sentence shone forth in §§3 and 9, and it does so again here. 'There's a rabbit' remains keyed to the sensory stimulations by which we learned it, even if we reinterpret the term 'rabbit' as denoting cosmic complements or singletons of rabbits. The term does continue to conjure up visions appropriate to the observation sentence through which the term was learned, and so be it; but there is no empirical bar to the reinterpretation. The original sensory associations were indispensable genetically in generating the nodes by which we structure our theory of the world. But all that matters by way of evidence for the theory is the stimulatory basis of the observation sentences plus the structure that the neutral nodes serve to implement. The stimulation remains as rabbity as ever, but the corresponding node or object goes neutral and is up for grabs.

Bodies were our primordial reifications, rooted in innate perceptual similarities. It would be gratuitous to swap them for proxies; the point was just that one could. But our ontological preconceptions have a less tenacious grip on the deliberate refinements of sophisticated science. Physicists did first picture elementary particles and light waves in analogy to familiar things, but they have gone on to sap the analogies. The particles are less and less like bodies, and the waves seem more like pulsations of energy in the void. When we get to the positing of numbers and other abstract objects, I have conjectured in *Roots of Reference* that we are indebted to some fruitful confusions along the way. Language and science are rooted in what good scientific language eschews. In Wittgenstein's figure, we climb the ladder and kick it away.

Some findings known as the Bose-Einstein and Fermi-Dirac statistics suggest how we might be led actually to repudiate even the more traditional elementary particles as values of variables, rather than retaining them and just acquiescing provisionally in their mysterious ways. Those results seem to show that there is no difference even in principle between saying of two elementary particles of a given kind that they are in the respective places *a* and *b* and that they are oppositely placed, in *b* and *a*. It would seem then not merely that elementary particles are unlike bodies; it would seem that there are no such denizens of space-time at all, and that we should speak of places *a* and *b* merely as being in certain states, indeed the same state, rather than as being occupied by two things.

Perhaps physicists will accommodate this quandary in another way. But I prize the example as illustrating the kind of consideration that could prompt one to repudiate some hypothetical objects. The consideration is not based on positivistic misgivings over theoretical entities. It is based on tensions internal to theory.

Theories can take yet more drastic turns: such not merely as to threaten a cherished ontology of elementary particles, but to threaten the very sense of the ontological question, the question what there is. What I have been taking as the standard idiom for existential purposes, namely quantification, can serve as standard only when embedded in the standard form of regimented language that we have been picturing: one whose further apparatus consists only of truth functions and predicates. If there is any deviation in this further apparatus, then there arises a question of foreign exchange: we cannot judge what existential content may be added by these foreign intrusions until we have settled on how to translate it all into our standard form. Notoriously, in particular, quantum mechanics invites logical deviations whose reduction to the old standard is by no means evident. On one rendering these deviations take the form of probabilistic predications. On an alternative rendering they call for basic departures from the logic of truth functions. When the dust has settled, we may find that the very notion of existence, the old one, has had its day. A kindred notion may then stand forth that seems sufficiently akin to warrant application of the same word; such is the way of terminology. Whether to say at that point that we have gained new insight into existence, or that we have outgrown the notion and reapplied the term, is a question of terminology as well.

The objectivity of our knowledge of the external world remains rooted in our contact with the external world, hence in our neural intake and the observation sentences that respond to it. We begin with the monolithic sentence, not the term. A lesson of proxy functions is that our ontology, like grammar, is part of our own conceptual contribution to our theory of the world. Man proposes; the world disposes, but only by holophrastic yes-or-no verdicts on the observation sentences that embody man's predictions.

III

MEANING

14. *The field linguist's entering wedge*

Philosophers in ancient India disputed over whether sentences or words were the primary vehicles of meaning. The argument in favor of words is that they are limited in number and can be learned once for all. Sentences are unlimited in number; we can fully master them only by learning how to construct them, as needed, from words learned in advance. Despite this situation, however, words can still be said to owe their meaning to their roles in sentences. We learn short sentences as wholes, we learn their component words from their use in those sentences, and we build further sentences from words thus learned. See §23.

The quest for a clear and substantial notion of meanings then should begin with an examination of sentences. The meaning of a sentence of one language is what it shares with its translations in another language, so I propounded my thought experiment of radical translation. It led to a negative conclusion, a thesis of indeterminacy of translation.

Critics have said that the thesis is a consequence of my behaviorism. Some have said that it is a *reductio ad absurdum* of my behaviorism. I disagree with this second point, but I agree with the first. I hold further that the behaviorist approach is mandatory. In psychology one may or may not be a behaviorist, but in linguistics one has no choice. Each of us learns his language by observing other people's verbal behavior and having his own faltering verbal behavior observed and reinforced or corrected by others. We depend strictly on overt behavior in observable situations. As long as our command of our language fits all external checkpoints, where our utterance or our reaction to someone's utterance can be appraised in the light of some shared situation, so long all is well. Our mental life between checkpoints is indifferent to our rating as a master of the language. There is nothing in linguistic meaning beyond what is to be gleaned from overt behavior in observable circumstances.

In my thought experiment the "source language," as the jargon has it, is Jungle; the "target language" is English. Jungle is inaccessible through any known languages as way stations, so our only data are native utterances and their outwardly observable circumstances. It is a meager basis, but the native speaker himself has had no other.

Our linguist would construct his manual of translation by conjectural extrapolation of such data, but the confirmations would be sparse. Usually the concurrent publicly observable situation does not enable us to predict what a speaker even of our own language will say, for utterances commonly bear little relevance to the circumstances outwardly observable at the time; there are ongoing projects and unshared past experiences. It is only thus, indeed, that language serves any useful communicative purpose; predicted utterances convey no news.

There are sentences, however, that do hinge pretty strictly on the concurrent publicly observable situation, namely the observation sentences. We saw these in Chapter I as the primary register of evidence about the external world, and also as the child's entering wedge into cognitive language. They are likewise the field linguist's entering wedge into the jungle language. Other utterances—greetings, commands, questions—will figure among the early acquisitions too, but the first declarative sentences to be mastered are bound to be observation sentences, and usually one word long. The linguist tentatively associates a native's utterance with the observed concurrent situation, hoping that it might be simply an observation sentence linked to that situation. To check this he takes the initiative, when the situation recurs, and volunteers the sentence himself for the native's assent or dissent.

This expedient of query and assent or dissent embodies, in miniature, the advantage of an experimental science such as physics over a purely observational science such as astronomy. To apply it the linguist must be able to recognize, if only conjecturally, the signs of assent and dissent in Jungle society. If he is wrong in guessing those signs, his further research will languish and he will try again. But there is a good deal to go on in identifying those signs. For one thing, a speaker will assent to an utterance in any curcumstance in which he would volunteer it.

What the native's observation sentence and the linguist's translation have in common, by this account, is the concurrent observable situation to which they are linked. But the notion of a situation has seemed too vague to rest with. In earlier writings I have accordingly represented the linguist as trying to match observation sentences of the jungle language with observation sentences of his own that have the

same stimulus meanings. That is to say, assent to the two
sentences should be prompted by the same stimulations;
likewise dissent.

15. *Stimulation again*

It would seem then that this matching of observation sentences hinges on sameness of stimulation of both parties,
the linguist and the informant. But an event of stimulation,
as I use the term (§1), is the activation of some subset of the
subject's sensory receptors. Since the linguist and his informant share no receptors, how can they be said to share a
stimulation? We might say rather that they undergo *similar*
stimulation, but that would assume still an approximate
homology of nerve endings from one individual to another.
Surely such anatomical minutiae ought not to matter here.

I was expressing this discomfort as early as 1965.[1] By
1981 it prompted me to readjust my definition of observation sentence. In my original definition I had appealed to
sameness of stimulus meaning between speakers,[2] but in
1981 I defined it rather for the single speaker, by the following condition:

> If querying the sentence elicits assent from the given speaker
> on one occasion, it will elicit assent likewise on any other
> occasion when the same total set of receptors is triggered;
> and similarly for dissent.[3]

Then I accounted a sentence observational for a whole community when it was observational for each member. In this

---

[1] E.g. in a lecture "Propositional Objects," published in *Ontological Relativity and Other Essays*.

[2] Thus *Word and Object*, p. 43.

[3] *Theories and Things*, p. 25.

way the question of intersubjective sameness of stimulation could be bypassed in studies of scientific method, I felt, and deferred to studies of translation. There it continued to rankle.

The question was much discussed in the course of a closed conference with Davidson, Dreben, and Føllesdal at Stanford in 1986.[4] Two years later, at the St. Louis conference on my philosophy,[5] Lars Bergström observed that even my bypassing of the question within studies of scientific method was unsuccessful, since a sentence could be observational for each of various speakers without their being disposed to assent to it in the same situations. It is odd that I overlooked this, for already in a lecture of 1974 I had remarked in effect that the fisherman's sentence 'I just felt a nibble' qualifies as observational for all individuals and not for the group.[6]

At the Stanford conference, Davidson proposed providing for intersubjective likeness of stimulation by locating the stimulus not at the bodily surface but farther out, in the nearest shared cause of the pertinent behavior of the two subjects. Failing a rabbit or other body to the purpose, perhaps the stimulus would be a shared situation, if ontological sense can be made of situations. But I remain unswerved in locating stimulation at the neural input, for my interest is epistemological, however naturalized. I am interested in the flow of evidence from the triggering of the senses to the pronouncements of science. My naturalism

[4] July 14–17, supported by Stanford's Center for the Study of Language and Information.

[5] "Perspectives on Quine," Washington University, April 9–13, 1988.

[6] "The Nature of Natural Knowledge," p. 72.

does allow *me* free reference to nerve endings, rabbits, and
other physical objects, so I could place the stimulus out
where Davidson does without finessing any reification on
the subject's part. But I am put off by the vagueness of
shared situations.

16. *To each his own*

The view that I have come to, regarding intersubjective
likeness of stimulation, is rather that we can simply do
without it. The observation sentence 'Rabbit' has its stimulus meaning for the linguist and 'Gavagai' has its for the
native, but the affinity of the two sentences is to be sought
in the externals of communication. The linguist notes the
native's utterance of 'Gavagai' where he, in the native's
position, might have said 'Rabbit'. So he tries bandying
'Gavagai' on occasions that would have prompted 'Rabbit',
and looks to natives for approval. Encouraged, he tentatively adopts 'Rabbit' as translation.

Empathy dominates the learning of language, both by
child and by field linguist. In the child's case it is the parent's
empathy. The parent assesses the appropriateness of the
child's observation sentence by noting the child's orientation and how the scene would look from there. In the field
linguist's case it is empathy on his own part when he makes
his first conjecture about 'Gavagai' on the strength of the
native's utterance and orientation, and again when he
queries 'Gavagai' for the native's assent in a promising subsequent situation. We all have an uncanny knack for empathizing another's peceptual situation, however ignorant
of the physiological or optical mechanism of his perception.

The knack is comparable, almost, to our ability to recognize faces while unable to sketch or describe them.

Empathy guides the linguist still as he rises above observation sentences through his analytical hypotheses (§17), though there he is trying to project into the native's associations and grammatical trends rather than his perceptions. And much the same must be true of the growing child.

As for the lacuna that Bergström noted, my definition of observation sentence in §2 reflects the correction in a rough and ready form. More fully: I retain my 1981 definition of observation sentence for the single speaker, and then account a sentence observational for a group if it is observational for each member *and* if each would agree in assenting to it, or dissenting, on witnessing the occasion of utterance. We judge what counts as witnessing the occasion, as in the translation case, by projecting ourselves into the witness's position.

A pioneer manual of translation has its utility as an aid to negotiation with the native community. Success in communication is judged by smoothness of conversation, by frequent predictability of verbal and nonverbal reactions, and by coherence and plausibility of native testimony. It is a matter of better and worse manuals rather than flatly right and wrong ones. Observation sentences continue to be the entering wedge for child and field linguist, and they continue to command the firmest agreement between rival manuals of translation; but their distinctive factuality is blurred now by the disavowal of shared stimulus meaning. What is utterly factual is just the fluency of conversation and the effectiveness of negotiation that one or another manual of translation serves to induce.

In *Word and Object* (p. 8) I pointed out that communication presupposes no similarity in nerve nets. Such was my parable of the trimmed bushes, alike in outward form but wildly unlike in their inward twigs and branches. The outward uniformity is imposed by society, in inculcating language and pressing for smooth communication. In a computer figure, we are dissimilar machines similarly programmed. Performance is mandated, implement it how one may. Such is the privacy of the nerve net. Dreben has likened it to the traditional privacy of other minds. Now in my new move I give the subject yet wider berth, allowing him the privacy even of his sensory receptors.

Unlike Davidson, I still locate the stimulations at the subject's surface, and private stimulus meanings with them. But they may be as idiosyncratic, for all I care, as the subject's internal wiring itself. What floats in the open air is our common language, which each of us is free to internalize in his peculiar neural way. Language is where intersubjectivity sets in. Communication is well named.

Obervation sentences are *stimulus-synonymous* for a speaker if their stimulus meanings are the same for him. But whereas one's stimulations and their ranges are a private affair, stimulus synonymy makes sense socially. Sentences are stimulus-synonymous for the community if stimulus-synonymous for each member. This still does not work between languages, unless the community is bilingual.

17. *Translation resumed*

Our linguist then goes on tentatively identifying and translating observation sentences. Some of them are perhaps compounded of others of them, in ways hinting of our logical particles 'and', 'or', 'but', 'not'. By collating the situations that command the natives' assent to the compounds with the situations that command assent to the components, and similarly for dissent, the linguist gets a plausible line on such connectives.

Unlike observation sentences, most utterances resist correlation with concurrent stimulations. Taking the initiative, the linguist may volunteer and query such a sentence for assent or dissent in various situations, but no correlation with concurrent stimulation is forthcoming. What next?

He can keep a record of these unconstrued sentences and dissect them. Some of the segments will have occurred also in the already construed observation sentences. He will treat them as words, and try pairing them off with English expressions in ways suggested by those observation sentences. Such are what I have called analytical hypotheses. There is guesswork here, and more extravagant guesswork to follow. The linguist will turn to the unconstrued, nonobservational sentences in which these same words occurred, and he will project conjectural interpretations of some of those sentences on the strength of these sporadic fragments. He will accumulate a tentative Jungle vocabulary, with English translations, and a tentative apparatus of grammatical constructions. Recursion then sets in, determining tentative translations of a potential infinity of sentences. Our linguist keeps testing his system for its efficacy in dealing with natives, and he goes on tinkering with it and guessing again. The routine of query and assent that had been his standby in construing observation sentences continues to be invaluable at these higher and more conjectural levels.

Clearly the task is formidable and the freedom for conjecture is enormous. Linguists can usually avoid radical translation by finding someone who can interpret the language, however haltingly, into a somewhat familiar one. But it is only radical translation that exposes the poverty of ultimate data for the identification of meanings.

Let us consider, then, what constraints our radical translator can bring to bear to help guide his conjectures. Continuity is helpful: successive utterances may be expected to have some bearing on one another. When several such have been tentatively interpreted, moreover, their interrelation itself may suggest the translation of a linking word that will be helpful in spotting similar connections elsewhere.

The translator will depend early and late on psychological conjectures as to what the native is likely to believe. This policy already governed his translations of observation sentences. It will continue to operate beyond the observational level, deterring him from translating a native assertion into too glaring a falsehood. He will favor translations that ascribe beliefs to the native that stand to reason or are consonant with the native's observed way of life. But he will not cultivate these values at the cost of unduly complicating the structure to be ascribed to the native's grammar and semantics, for this again would be bad psychology; the language must have been simple enough for acquisition by the natives, whose minds, failing evidence to the contrary, are presumed to be pretty much like our own. Practical psychology is what sustains our radical translator all along the way, and the method of his psychology is empathy: he imagines himself in the native's situation as best he can.

Our radical translator would put his developing manual of translation continually to use, and go on revising it in the light of his successes and failures of communication. The successes consist—to repeat—in successful negotiation and smooth conversation. Reactions of astonishment or bewilderment on a native's part, or seemingly irrelevant responses, tend to suggest that the manual has gone wrong.

We readily imagine the translator's ups and downs. Perhaps he has tentatively translated two native sentences into English ones that are akin to each other in some semantic way, and he finds this same kinship reflected in a native's use of the two native sentences. This encourages him in his pair of tentative translations. So he goes on blithely supposing that he is communicating, only to be caught up short. This may persuade him that his pair of translations was wrong after all. He wonders how far back, in the smooth-flowing antecedent conversation, he got off the beam.

18. Indeterminacy of translation

Considerations of the sort we have been surveying are all that the radical translator has to go on. This is not because the meanings of sentences are elusive or inscrutable; it is because there is nothing to them, beyond what these fumbling procedures can come up with. Nor is there hope even of codifying these procedures and then *defining* what counts as translation by citing the procedures; for the procedures involve weighing incommensurable values. How much grotesqueness may we allow to the native's beliefs, for instance, in order to avoid how much grotesqueness in his grammar or semantics?

These reflections leave us little reason to expect that two radical translators, working independently on Jungle, would come out with interchangeable manuals. Their manuals might be indistinguishable in terms of any native behavior that they give reason to expect, and yet each manual might prescribe some translations that the other translator would reject. Such is the thesis of indeterminacy of translation.

A manual of Jungle-to-English translation constitutes a recursive, or inductive, definition of a *translation relation* together with a claim that it correlates sentences compatibly with the behavior of all concerned. The thesis of indeterminacy of translation is that these claims on the part of two manuals might both be true and yet the two translation relations might not be usable in alternation, from sentence to sentence, without issuing in incoherent sequences. Or, to put it another way, the English sentences prescribed as translation of a given Jungle sentence by two rival manuals might not be interchangeable in English contexts.

The use of one or the other manual might indeed cause differences in speech afterward, as remarked by Robert Kirk in connection with the idioms of propositional attitude; but the two would do equal justice to the status quo.

I have directed my indeterminacy thesis on a radically exotic language for the sake of plausibility, but in principle it applies even to the home language. For given the rival manuals of translation between Jungle and English, we can translate English perversely into English by translating it into Jungle by one manual and then back by the other.

The indeterminacy of translation is unlikely to obtrude in practice, even in radical translation. There is good reason why it should not. The linguist assumes that the native's attitudes and ways of thinking are like his own, up to the point where there is contrary evidence. He accordingly imposes his own ontology and linguistic patterns on the native wherever compatible with the native's speech and other

behavior, unless a contrary course offers striking simplifications. We could not wish otherwise. What the indeterminacy thesis is meant to bring out is that the radical translator
is bound to impose about as much as he discovers.

19. Syntax

Readers have supposed that I extended my indeterminacy
thesis to syntax. This puzzled me until I became aware,
recently, of a subtle cause of the misconception. In *Word and
Object* (pp. 55, 68–72) I claimed that our distinctive apparatus of reification and reference is subject to indeterminacy of translation. The apparatus includes pronouns, ' = ',
plural endings, indeed whatever serves the logical purposes
of quantifiers and variables. But these devices, some of my
readers have reasoned, are part of what syntax is about. So
indeterminacy, they have supposed, extends to syntax.

The business of syntax is the demarcation of strings of
phonemes proper to the language. More than one battery of
grammatical constructions and vocabulary will probably be
capable of generating the same total output of strings, but in
this freedom there is no indeterminacy analogous to that of
translation. Indeterminacy of translation consists rather in
conflict in the outputs themselves.[7]

What misled those readers was the indeterminacy of
translation of pronouns and other referential devices. But
that indeterminacy was only over whether to equate certain
Jungle locutions to these devices or to something else. The
translator will accommodate those locutions anyway,

[7] The syntactician may indeed exercise some freedom in setting the
limits of the language, but only marginally. See *From a Logical Point of
View*, pp. 53–55.

whatever his translations. He may or may not call them pronouns, plurals, quantifiers, and so on, according as he thinks in terms of one or another manual of translation. The difference will be only verbal or, at most, a choice of one syntactic structure rather than another for generating one and the same total output of Jungle strings.

20. Indeterminacy of reference

The difference between taking a sentence holophrastically as a seamless whole and taking it analytically term by term proved crucial in earlier matters (§§3, 9, 13). It is crucial also to translation. Taken analytically, the indeterminacy of translation is trivial and indisputable. It was factually illustrated in *Ontological Relativity* (pp. 35–36) by the Japanese classifiers, and more abstractly above by proxy functions (§13). It is the unsurprising reflection that divergent interpretations of the words in a sentence can so offset one another as to sustain an identical translation of the sentence as a whole. It is what I have called inscrutability of reference; 'indeterminacy of reference' would have been better. The serious and controversial thesis of indeterminacy of translation is not that; it is rather the holophrastic thesis, which is stronger. It declares for divergences that remain unreconciled even at the level of the whole sentence, and are compensated for only by divergences in the translations of other whole sentences.

Unlike indeterminacy of reference, which is so readily illustrated by mutually compensatory adjustments within the limits of a single sentence, the full or holophrastic indeterminacy of translation draws too broadly on a language to admit of factual illustration. Radical translation is a rare achievement, and it is not going to be undertaken successfully twice for the same language. But see Levy for a plausible artificial example, based on measurement in deviant geometries. Also there is Massey's sweeping example based on the duality of affirmation to negation, conjunction to alternation, and universal quantification to existential. His rival translations, the homophonic and its dual, conflict on every sentence. A weakness of this construction is that the dual manual depends on viewing the natives' volunteered sentences as denied rather than affirmed—a gratuitous reversal of the translator's conventional orientation. Still, in view of Levy's construction if not Massey's, one can scarcely question the holophrastic indeterminacy thesis.

A thick and imposing periodical on the philosophy of language is published twice a year in the Canary Islands under the title *Gavagai*. A book by David Premack, on his language experiments with chimpanzees, came out lately under the title *Gavagai*. Hubert Dreyfus has California vanity plates on his Volkswagen Rabbit that spell 'GAVAGAI'. The word has become the logo of my thesis of indeterminacy of translation, and now it is making its way in a wider world. Ironically, indeterminacy of translation in the strong sense was not what I coined the word to illustrate. It did not illustrate that, for 'Gavagai' is an observation sentence, firmly translatable holophrastically as '(Lo, a) rabbit'. But this translation is insufficient to fix the reference of 'gavagai' as a term; that was the point of the example. It is an extreme example of the indeterminacy of reference, the contained term being the whole of the sentence. No room is left here for compensatory adjustments, and none are needed.

Kindly readers have sought a technical distinction between my phrases 'inscrutability of reference' and 'ontological relativity' that was never clear in my own mind. But I can now say what ontological relativity is relative to, more succinctly than I did in the lectures, paper, and book of that title. It is relative to a manual of translation. To say that 'gavagai' denotes rabbits is to opt for a manual of translation in which 'gavagai' is translated as 'rabbit', instead of opting for any of the alternative manuals.

And does the indeterminacy or relativity extend also somehow to the home language? In "Ontological Relativity" I said it did, for the home language can be translated into itself by permutations that depart materially from the mere identity transformation, as proxy functions bear out. But if we choose as our manual of translation the identity transformation, thus taking the home language at face value, the relativity is resolved. Reference is then explicated in disquotational paradigms analogous to Tarski's truth paradigm (§33); thus 'rabbit' denotes rabbits, whatever *they* are, and 'Boston' designates Boston.

21. Whither meanings?

If we could contrive an acceptable relation of sameness of meaning, it would be a short step to an acceptable definition of meanings. For, as more than one philosopher has noted, we could define the meaning of an expression as the class of all expressions like it in meaning. Conversely, if we had the meanings to begin with, they and identity would provide sameness of meaning, there being no entity without identity.[8] In short, meanings and sameness of meaning present one and the same problem.

[8] This platitude has lately been obscured by a confusion over the axiom of extensionality, which individuates sets, or classes, and has been suspended by some set theorists in an exploratory spirit. Might we not likewise recognize meanings without identity? No. Dropping extension-

Translation does enjoy reasonable determinacy up through observation categoricals and into the logical connectives. Thus one could make a stab at the interlinguistic equating of empirical content (§7), even in radical translation. But empirical content pertains only to testable sentences and sets of sentences. We are still left with no general concept of the meanings of sentences of less than critical semantic mass.

It is not a conclusion that one readily jumps to or rests with. One is tempted to suppose that we might define meanings for sentences of less than critical mass, and even for terms, by substitutivity. If we can interchange two expressions without disturbing the empirical content of any testable context, are they not alike in meaning? Well, the plan collapses between languages. Interchanging expressions would turn the context into nonsense if the expressions belong to different languages. So the plan offers no relief from the indeterminacy of translation.

22. Domestic meaning

Lowering our sights, then, and giving up on "propositions" as language-transcendent sentence meanings, we might still look to the substitutivity expedient for a strictly domestic, interlinguistically inapplicable notion of sameness of meaning. Sentences are *cognitively equivalent,* we might say, if putting one for the other does not affect the empirical content of any set of sentences. This sounds right in principle. For the most part it resists decisive application,

---

ality does not exempt sets from identity either. It only tables the question of sufficient conditions for their identity. The notation '$x = y$' stays on, with sets as values of the variables. There is still no entity—no set, nothing—without identity.

however, because of the rather visionary status of empirical content (§7).

Another approach looks to belief: to the speaker's assent or dissent when the sentences are queried. This would not do for standing sentences; it would equate all his beliefs. But it works for occasion sentences, where we can check each pair for concomitance over varying occasions. Two occasion sentences may be accounted cognitively equivalent for a given speaker if he is disposed on every occasion to assent to both or dissent from both or abstain. Derivatively, then, they may be accounted cognitively equivalent for the community if cognitively equivalent for each member. When in particular the sentences are observation sentences, we are back to stimulus synonymy (§16).

Cognitive equivalence so defined then extends immediately to terms, or predicates. They are cognitively equivalent, or we might now say cognitively *synonymous,* if their predications—'It's an F', 'It's a G'—are cognitively equivalent. In view of our definition of cognitive equivalence of occasion sentences, this boils down to saying that terms are cognitively synonymous for a speaker if he believes them to be coextensive, that is, true of the same things; and synonymous for the community if synonymous for each member.

Some slight progress can then be made toward cognitive equivalence of standing sentences. Certainly they should be rated cognitively equivalent if one can be got from the other by supplanting a component term by a cognitive synonym. But this does not cover all the pairs of standing sentences that we would want to regard as cognitively equivalent.

There is a third approach in *analyticity*. Once we have analyticity, cognitive equivalence is forthcoming; for two sentences are cognitively equivalent if and only if their truth-functional biconditional is analytic. Now a sentence is analytic, in mentalistic semantics, when it is true by virtue of the meanings of its words. In *Roots of Reference* (pp. 70–80) I suggested externalizing the criterion: a sentence is analytic if the native speaker learns to assent to it by learning one or more of its words. This accounts for such paradigms of analyticity as 'No bachelor is married', and also for the analyticity of many elementary logical truths. The concept can be adjusted to cover also the truths derivable from analytic truths by analytic steps.

I think this definition does some justice to the intuitive notion of tautology, the notion that comes into play when we protest that someone's assertion comes down to '0 = 0' and is an empty matter of words. But the definition gives no clue to the demarcation between analytic and synthetic sentences that has exercised philosophers, out beyond where anyone either remembers or cares how he learned the pertinent words. And it gives no clue, certainly, to a general concept of cognitive equivalence.

Why was it important? Where metaphysics had sought the essence of things, analytical philosophy as of G. E. Moore and after settled for the meanings of words; but still it was as if there were intrinsic meanings to be teased out rather than just fluctuant usage to be averaged out. Analyticity, then, reflected the meanings of words as metaphysical necessity had reflected the essences of things. In later years analyticity served Carnap in his philosophy of mathematics, explaining how mathematics could be meaningful despite lacking empirical content, and why it is necessarily true. However, holism settles both questions without appeal to analyticity. Holism lets mathematics share empirical content where it is applied, and it accounts for mathematical necessity by freedom of selection and the maxim of minimum mutilation (§6).

23. Lexicography

To question the old notion of meanings of words and sentences is not to repudiate semantics. Much good work has been done regarding the manner, circumstances, and development of the use of words. Lexicography is its conspicuous manifestation. But I would not seek a scientific rehabilitation of something like the old notion of separate and distinct meanings; that notion is better seen as a stumbling block cleared away. In later years indeed it has been more of a stumbling block for philosophers than for scientific linguists, who, understandably, have simply found it not technically useful.

Dictionaries are reputedly occupied with explaining the meanings of words, and the work is neither myth-bound nor capricious. How does it proceed? I hold that it is not directed at cognitive equivalence of sentences, nor at synonymy of terms, and that it presupposes no notion of meaning at all. Let us consider then what the business of dictionaries really is.

Sometimes the dictionary explains a word by supplying another expression that can replace it *salva veritate* at least in positions uncontaminated by quotation or idioms of propositional attitude. Sometimes, instead, a selection of information is set down regarding the object or objects to which the word refers. There is no pretense here of a distinction between essential and accidental traits. It is a matter purely of pedagogy: the lexicographer wants to improve his reader's chances of successful communication as best he can in a small compass. Often, moreover, a dictionary entry neither paraphrases the word nor describes its objects, but describes, rather, the use of the word in sentences. This is usually the way with grammatical particles, and it is often the way also with terms. It is bound to be the way with a term that neither refers to concrete objects nor admits of a separable, self-contained paraphrase.

Behind this seeming disorder there is a unifying principle. The goal may be seen always as the sentence. The lexicographer is out to help his reader profit by the sentences that he sees or hears, and to help him react to them in expected ways, and to help him emit sentences usefully. But sentences are unlimited in their variety, so the lexicographer organizes his teaching of sentences word by word, teaching how to use each word in making sentences. One way of teaching this, which is convenient when available, is by citing a substitute expression; for the lexicographer thus exploits the reader's presumed knowledge of how to use that substitute expression in making sentences. And the other sorts of dictionary entry likewise aim, in their different ways, at the same end: teaching the use of sentences.

When from semantics as pursued by philosophers we move to lexicography, we shift our focus from likeness of meaning to knowledge of meaning, so to speak; from synonymy of expressions, anyway, to the understanding of expressions. The lexicographer's job is to inculcate understanding of expressions, that is, to teach how to use them. He can be wholly successful in teaching the use of sentences without considering in what sense they might be said to be equivalent. Nothing, apparently, could be more remote than meanings from the lexicographer's concern. Why should they be less remote from ours?

So we might try looking to the understanding of expressions, rather than to synonymy, as the operationally basic notion of semantics. What sense can we make of it? In practice we credit someone with understanding a sentence if we are not surprised by the circumstances of his uttering it or by his reaction to hearing it—provided further that his reaction is not one of visible bewilderment. We suspect that he does not understand it if the event is drastically at variance with those conditions. Still no boundary is evident, no general criterion for deciding whether he actually misunderstands the sentence or merely holds some unusual theory regarding its subject matter.

We can be more confident in imputing misunderstanding of a word than of a sentence, for we can then observe someone's use of numerous sentences, or his response to them, all of which contain the word. We can control our experiment, choosing and querying sentences ourselves. We may find that he responds otherwise than would generally be expected when the sentences contain the word in question, and that he responds in the more usual ways to many sentences that lack that word but are much the same in other respects.

In this matter of understanding language there is thus a subtle interplay between word and sentence. In one way the sentence is fundamental: understanding a word consists in knowing how to use it in sentences and how to react to such sentences. Yet if we would test someone's understanding of a sentence, we do best to focus on a word, ringing changes on its sentential contexts. Once we have thus satisfied ourselves, through a multiplicity of such sentences, that he misunderstands the word, we are justified at last in concluding that his odd response to the original sentence containing it was due to a misunderstanding of the word and not to some odd opinion regarding matters of fact.

Understanding, behaviorally viewed, is thus a statistical effect: it resides in multiplicities. The nucleus is the word, and the mass is made up of the countless sentences in which the word occurs. A predominantly healthy or unhealthy coloring of this mass is what counts as understanding or misunderstanding of the word and the sentences; and a sharp boundary need not be sought. A forest presents a sharp boundary to the airborne observer but not to the man on the ground; an ink blot presents a sharp outline to the unaided eye and not under a magnifying glass; and we can acquiesce in a similar attitude toward the distinction between understanding and misunderstanding an expression. Lexicography has no need of synonymy, we saw, and it has no need of a sharp distinction between understanding and misunderstanding either. The lexicographer's job is to improve his reader's understanding of expressions, but he can get on with that without drawing a boundary. He does what he can, within a limited compass, to adjust the reader's verbal behavior to that of the community as a whole, or of some preferred quarter of it. The adjustment is a matter of degree, and a vague one: a matter of fluency and effectiveness of dialogue.

IV

INTENSION

24. Perception and observation sentences

Observation sentences, typically, are reports of events or situations in the external world. Some are mentalistic, however, and they can play an important role. Thus consider, to begin with, the observation sentence 'It's raining'. Tom is learning it from Martha by ostension. Martha's business is to encourage Tom in uttering the sentence, or in assenting to it, when she sees that he is noticing appropriate phenomena, and to discourage him otherwise. Thus Tom's mastery of the physicalistic sentence 'It's raining' hinges on Martha's mastery, virtual if not literal, of the mentalistic sentence 'Tom perceives that it's raining'.

Observation sentences, learned ostensively, are where our command of language begins, and our learning them from our elders depends heavily on the ability of our elders to guess that we are getting the appropriate perception. The handing down of language is thus implemented by a continuing command, tacit at least, of the idiom 'x perceives that p' where 'p' stands for an observation sentence. Command of this mentalistic notion would seem therefore to be about as old as language. It is remarkable that the bifurcation between physicalistic and mentalistic talk is foreshadowed already at the level of observation sentences, as between 'It is raining' and 'Tom perceives that it is raining'. Man is indeed a forked animal.

Each perception that it is raining is a fleeting neural event. Two perceptions by Tom that it is raining are apt to differ, moreover, not only in time of occurrence but neurally, because there are varied indicators of rain. Tom's perceptions of its raining constitute a class of events that is perhaps too complex and heterogeneous neurally to be practically describable in neurological terms even given full knowledge of the facts. Yet there is also, we may be sure, some neural trait that unites these neural events as a class; for it was by stimulus generalization, or subjective similarity, that Tom eventually learned to make the observation sentence 'It's raining' do for all of them.

So much for Tom. The class of the whole population's perceptions of its raining will be much more forbidding still, since people's nerve nets differ—certainly in consequence of different histories of learning, and perhaps genetically as well. Yet the idiom 'perceives that it's raining' cuts through all that hopeless neurological complexity and encapsulates all perception that it is raining—not just on Tom's part, but on everyone's.

It does so by citing a symptom rather than a neural mechanism. And what a remarkable sort of symptom! We detect it by empathetic observation of the subject's facial expressions and what is happening in front of him, perhaps, and we specify it by a content clause consisting of a vicarious observation sentence.

Martha empathizes Tom's perception that it is raining just as the field linguist empathizes the native's perception that a rabbit has appeared (§16). Learning a language in the field and teaching it in the nursery are much the same at the

level of observation sentences: a matter of perceiving that
the subject is perceiving that p.

25. Perception extended

Observationality varies with the group of speakers concerned, and is also, within the group, somewhat a matter of
degree (§2). Consequently the construction 'perceives that
p' continues to flourish when the content clause is not observational, or not very. We even hear 'Tom perceives that the
train is late'.

Consider how one would get on to using that sentence.
People have ways of showing that they perceive that the
train is late, and these ways run to type. One way is by
saying that the train is late. Also people pace impatiently,
they look at the clock, they look along the track. Along
with acquiring such habits ourselves, we have learned to
observe similar manifestations on the part of others. We are
ready to see our own ways replicated in another person.
This readiness was what enabled us to teach observation
sentences to other persons, and to learn when to affirm 'x
perceives that p' in observational cases; and the ability extends beyond observation sentences to sentences like 'The
train is late'.

The evidence is not assembled deliberately. One empathizes, projecting oneself into Tom's situation and Tom's
behavior pattern, and finds thereby that the sentence 'The
train is late' is what comes naturally. Such is the somewhat
haphazard basis for saying that Tom perceives that the train
is late. The basis becomes more conclusive if the observed
behavior on Tom's part includes a statement of his own that
the train is late.

An occasion sentence of the form '*x* perceives that *p*' can be true even when the content clause is a standing sentence, such as 'Randy is a dog', rather than an occasion sentence. What is then required, however, is not only that the percipient be prepared on that occasion to assent to that clause, but also that he be just then becoming aware that it is true. Ascriptions of perceptions call increasingly for background knowledge and conjecture on the ascriptor's part as we move away from observation sentences.

26. *Perception of things*

Alongside the construction '*x* perceives that *p*', where the perception is described by a content clause, we have the construction '*x* perceives *y*', where the perception is described by a term as objective complement. The term designates an object that incites sensory receptors that arouse the percipient's attention. If the object is a bowl, the force may be the light that it reflects to the eye. But that light is coming also from the sun, or from a lamp, via the bowl. What distinguishes the perceived object is perhaps that the force comes from it directly? No, this will not do; we want also to allow the bowl to be perceived by reflection in a mirror.

There is an easy solution: *focus*. Between perceiving the bowl reflected in the glass and perceiving the glass itself there is a difference in the tension of the eye muscles; for the focal distance of the bowl is the total distance from the eye to the glass and thence to the bowl. The same criterion of focus serves to distinguish between seeing something through a glass and seeing the glass.

But focal distance and causality do not suffice to single out the perceived object. A bit of the surface of the bowl would meet those conditions as well as the bowl itself. Anything of which that patch of surface is a part would likewise qualify—thus the bowl, or the nearer half of the bowl, or any sector of the environment that includes the bowl, taken over any period of time that includes the stimulatory event. Which of these objects to count as perceived would be settled by the percipient's observation sentence, if he were to volunteer one.[1]

We noted earlier (§§3, 9, 13) that observation terms, retrospectively seen as designating objects, are best viewed at their inception rather as one-word observation sentences. The same attitude best befits the ascription of perceptions: think of 'x perceives y' in the image rather of 'x perceives that p'. We say 'Tom perceives the bowl' because in empathizing Tom's situation we fancy ourselves volunteering the observation sentence 'Bowl' rather than 'Surface of a bowl', 'Front half of a bowl', 'Bowl and background'.

Adherence to content clauses, in preference to perceived objects, imposes no real restraint on our day-to-day ascriptions of perception. When we ask 'What did he perceive?' we are content with an answer of the form 'He perceived that p'. When we say 'They perceived the same thing' a fuller explanation in the form 'They perceived that p' affords satisfaction. The stubbornly substantival 'What' and 'same thing' intrude only for lack of words to stand for clauses.

27. Belief and perception

The idiom 'x perceives that p' applies beyond observation sentences, we saw, and even beyond occasion sentences

[1] For further quandaries about perceived objects see Chisholm, ch 10.

altogether. Usage pushes it, indeed, to all heights. One is even said to perceive that Newton's laws imply Kepler's. But with all this extension of usage, one requirement continues to be respected: we are said to perceive that *p* only on the occasion when we first learn that *p*. When this condition is dropped, we speak no longer of perception in any sense; we speak of belief.

An ascription '*x* perceives that *p*' is still an occasion sentence even when its content clause is a standing sentence; for a perception is still a momentary event. On the other hand an ascription '*x* believes that *p*' is a standing sentence, a belief being an enduring state.

Other differences, mere accidents of usage, may be noted in passing. A perception is an event in just one percipient and at just one time, though he may undergo others just like it; a belief, on the other hand, can have many believers. Perceptions are treated as veridical, beliefs not: we do not perceive that *p* unless *p*, but we can mistakenly believe that *p*.

The kinship is more significant. When we ascribe a perception, in the idiom '*x* perceives that *p*', our evidence consists in observing the percipient's orientation and behavior and appreciating that we in his place would feel prompted to volunteer the content clause ourselves. When we ascribe a belief in the idiom '*x* believes that *p*', our evidence is similar but usually more tenuous. We reflect on the believer's behavior, verbal and otherwise, and what we know of his past, and conjecture that we in his place would feel prepared to assent, overtly or covertly, to the content clause.

Asking is the easiest way of determining someone's belief, though questions of sincerity and translation can arise.

A wager is a good test when the belief is of the sort where a bet can eventually be settled. Arguments offered in support of a belief are a further sign, however inconclusive, of holding it. Some beliefs are evinced by flight, by bathing, by tidying up the parlor. Manifestations of belief vary extravagantly with the belief and the circumstances of the believer.

We saw in §25 that ascriptions of perception get more tenuous and conjectural as we move from observational content clauses to others and finally to standing ones. Ascriptions of belief run more tenuous still, and their supporting evidence is diffuse. The ascription of beliefs by content clauses is disarming in its syntax: any declarative sentence is grammatically admissible as content clause, and hence is presumed to yield an intelligible ascription, however remote from any conceivable evidence. A belief can be as firmly testified in behavior as a tail-wagging dog's belief that his dinner is forthcoming. But what are we to say of a belief in the transubstantiation of the eucharist?

The construction 'perceives that p' was essential to the propagation of language (§24), and at that observational level it was well under the control of empirical evidence. By extrapolation, analogy, and further extrapolation, however, it has spawned a boundless, lawless swarm: the ascriptions of belief. Responsible ones grade off into the irresponsible, and one despairs of drawing a line.

28. Propositional attitudes

In 'perceives that p' and 'believes that p' we have two among many idioms of *propositional attitude*. Others are 'hopes that p', 'regrets that p', 'fears that p', 'strives that p', 'wonders whether p', and indeed 'says that p'. Empathy figures in most ascriptions of these kinds, to subjects other than oneself. This is true even of 'says that p': the allowable departures from direct quotation depend on what the ascriber deems the quoted subject to have had in mind. Whether to paraphrase 'the commissioner' as 'that scoundrel', in an indirect quotation, is a question not of the commissioner's character, but of the quoted speaker's view of it.

Empathy is why we ascribe a propositional attitude by a content clause. We saw (§26) that content clauses were more to the point than terms as grammatical objects even in the case of perception. The content clause purports to reflect the subject's state of mind rather than the state of things. From the ascriber's point of view it figures holophrastically; its component terms do not necessarily refer, here, as he means them to when he speaks for himself.

The objects of propositional attitudes—what are believed, regretted, etc.—have commonly been taken to be propositions, or sentence meanings; but these have gone by the board (§21). I take them simply as sentences, namely the content clauses themselves, thus treating 'that' as a quotation mark initiating a name of what comes after it. Obvious adjustments are to be understood in cases like 'He believes he is Napoleon'; the belief is 'I am Napoleon.'

In thus ascribing propositional attitudes to men and beasts by quotation I do not ascribe a command of the quoted language, or of any. A cat can believe 'A mouse is in there'. The language is that of the ascriber of the attitude, though he projects it empathetically to the creature in the attitude. The cat is purportedly in a state of mind in which the ascriber *would* say 'A mouse is in there'. The quotational account reflects the empathy that invests the idioms of propositional attitude from 'perceives that' onward.

If we were to activate this account by actually rewriting the 'that' as quotation, rather than just noting it as tacit intent, we would confound indirect quotation with direct. But we could easily resolve the ambiguity by agreeing to distinguish two verbs: 'say' for indirect quotation, 'utter' for direct, and quotation marks for both.

We are familiar with the failure of substitutivity of identity in content clauses of propositional attitude. It fails because the person in the attitude may be unaware of the pertinent identity. This failure was a concern of Frege's. Likewise we must beware of quantifying into such a clause, for the values of the variable of our outlying quantifier are the things of our real world, and might not fit the attitudinist's ontology. Such is the referential opacity of the propositional attitudes. The quotational account nicely dramatizes it, for the quotation designates a mere string of phonemes or signs, whose syntax and semantics, if any, are a strictly internal affair.

Not that we must acquiesce in the quotation as a syntactically indigestible mass relative to the broader context. It is digestible by spelling. We adopt names for all single signs, finite in number, and then generate a name of any string of signs by intercalating a sign of concatenation. Thus 'παν' is pi⌢alpha⌢nu, and this is as straightforward in its syntax as arithmetical addition or a polynomial.

Spelling dissolves the syntax and lexicon of the content clause and blends it with that of the ascriber's language. So long as we rest with the unanalyzed quotational form, on the other hand, the inverted commas mark an opaque interface between two ontologies, two worlds: that of the man in the attitude, however benighted, and that of our responsible ascriber of the attitude.

The interface is sometimes breached. Like an actor stepping out of his part and speaking for himself, the ascriber is heard to say of the real people of his world that

(1)   There are some whom Ralph believes to be spies,

not just that

(2)   Ralph believes '$\exists x(x$ is a spy)'.

If rendered quotationally, (1) goes incoherent.

(3) $\exists x$(Ralph believes 'x is a spy').

The quotation in (3) is just a name of a string of seven letters and three spaces; its 'x' has nothing to do with the outlying '$\exists x$'. (1) ascribed belief *de re;* quotation ascribes it *de dicto.*

Between (1) and (2) we sense the vital difference between spotting a suspect and merely believing, like all of us, that there are spies. In affirming (1) we dissociate Ralph's suspicions from the world as he conceives it and train them upon denizens of our real world; we ride roughshod over failures of identification on his part. Ralph suspects a man whom he has seen lurking about a certain sensitive installation; meanwhile he esteems Bernard J. Ortcutt as a pillar of society. He is unaware that they are the same man. Does he then both suspect Ortcutt and think him innocent? That would be impossible or, at best, unfair to Ralph.[2]

Propositional attitudes *de re* presuppose a relation of *intention,* between thoughts and things intended, for which I

---

[2]Accommodation of (1) by singular descriptions was refuted by Sleigh, *q.v.*

conceive of no adequate guidelines. To garner empirical content for (1) we would have to interrogate Ralph and compile some of his pertinent beliefs *de dicto*.

I conclude that the propositional attitudes *de re* resist annexation to scientific language, as propositional attitudes *de dicto* do not. At best the ascriptions *de re* are signals pointing a direction in which to look for informative ascriptions *de dicto*.

29. *Anomalous monism*

We reflected in §24 that a neurological rendering of 'Tom perceives that it is raining', applicable to all such occasions merely on Tom's part, would already be pretty formidable even if Tom's neural make-up were known in detail. We reflected further that a neurological rendering of 'perceives that it is raining', applicable to all comers, would be out of the question.

Yet each perception is a single occurrence in a particular brain, and is fully specifiable in neurological terms once the details are known. We cannot say the same for a belief, which can be publicly shared, but we can say somewhat the same for the instance of the belief in a single believer. The period during which I go on believing that the earth rotates is distinguished from my earlier stages by at least some verbal dispositions, which must reside in some distinctive quirks in my nervous system.

Perceptions are neural realities, and so are the individual instances of beliefs and other propositional attitudes insofar as these do not fade out into irreality altogether (§27). Physicalistic explanation of neural events and states goes blithely forward with no intrusion of mental laws or intensional concepts. What are irreducibly mental are ways of grouping them: grouping a lot of respectably physical perceptions as perceptions that p, and grouping a lot of respectably physical belief instances as the belief that p. I acquiesce in what Davidson calls anomalous monism, also known as token physicalism: there is no mental substance, but there are irreducibly mental ways of grouping physical states and events.

At first the problem of mind was ontological and linguistic. With the passing of mind as substance, there remained a twofold problem of mentalistic language: syntactic and semantic. The distinctive syntactic trait of mentalistic discourse was the content clause, 'that p'. This obstructed *extensionality*: that is, the substitutivity of identity and more generally the interchangeability of all coextensive terms and clauses *salva veritate*. It obstructed classical predicate logic as a universal theoretical framework. Now this quarter of the mind problem is in a fair way to dissolution. Quotational treatment of propositional attitudes *de dicto* delivers them to the extensional domain of predicate logic, thanks to the reduction of quotation to spelling. Propositional attitudes *de re*, on the other hand, we downgraded.

So we see the attitudes *de dicto* reconciled syntactically with extensional logic. A single language, regimented in predicate logic, can take them in stride along with natural science. The residual oddity of these mentalistic predicates *de dicto* is purely semantic: they do not interlock productively with the self-sufficient concepts and causal laws of natural science.

Still the mentalistic predicates, for all their vagueness (§27), have long interacted with one another, engendering age-old strategies for predicting and explaining human action. They complement natural science in their incommensurable way, and are indispensable both to the social sciences and to our everyday dealings. Read Dennett and Davidson.

30. Modalities

The modalities of necessity and possibility are not overtly mentalistic, but still they are intensional, in the sense of resisting substitutivity of identity. Here again we have the interplay between *de dicto* and *de re*. Thus 'nec (7 < the number of the planets)' is true *de re,* since nec (7 < 9), but false *de dicto.*

In respect of utility there is less to be said for necessity than for the propositional attitudes. The expression does serve a purpose in daily discourse, but of a shallow sort. We modify a sentence with the adverb 'necessarily' when it is a sentence presumed acceptable to our interlocutor and stated only as a step toward the consideration of moot ones. Or we write 'necessarily' to identify something that follows from generalities already expounded, as over against new conjectures or hypotheses. Such utility is local, transitory, and unproblematic, like the utility of indexical expressions. The sublimity of necessary truth turns thus not quite to dust, but to pretty common clay.

The subjunctive or contrary-to-fact conditional has had close associations with the necessity idiom, and a similar account of it expresses almost a commonsense view. The conditional holds if its consequent follows logically from its antecedent in conjunction with background sentences that one's interlocutor is prepared to grant, or sentences that one has already set down or implicitly assumed in one's expository piece. The consequent of the conditional follows from the antecedent *ceteris paribus,* and those supporting sentences are the *cetera paria.*

Chatting of sublimity and common clay, I might pause for a word on essence. Champions of modal logic mean necessity to have an objective sense, as if to say metaphysical necessity or physical necessity. But then it must make sense to speak of a thing's essence, comprising those properties that it has necessarily. For, 'x necessarily has F' is simply 'nec Fx'. The essence has to be *de re,* inherent in the thing independently of how referred to, since the thing can figure simply as the value of a neutral variable as here.

In its everyday use as I described it, 'necessarily' is a second-order annotation to the effect that its sentence is deemed true by all concerned, at least for the sake and space of the argument. A similar second-order role is cut out, then, for 'possibly'. Since it simply means 'not necessarily not', 'possibly' marks its sentence as one that the beliefs or working assumptions of concerned parties do not exclude as false. Thanks to our overwhelming ignorance, the realm of possibility thus conceived is vaster far than that of necessity. It is the domain of all our plans and conjectures, all our hopes and fears.

31. *A mentalistic heritage*

Appreciation of one another's perceptions is fundamental, we saw (§24), to the handing down of language. The mentalistic strain is thus archaic. We see it in animism, the primitive ascription of minds to bodies on an excessive scale. Perhaps there was a vestige of animism in Aristotle's theory of the natural motion of substances: earth down-

ward, fire upward, stars around and around. We see the
archaic dominance of mentalism in a preference for final
cause over efficient cause as a mode of explanation. It is
evident in the Middle Ages. The bestiaries accounted for the
supposed traits or practices of various animals as God's way
of setting moral examples for man to emulate. This predi-
lection for explanation by final cause is evident still today in
people who seek the meaning of life. They want to explain
life by finding its purpose.

Purpose is one of various mentalistic notions drawn from
introspection of one's mental life. Others are disposition
and capability. All three reflect one's sense of will, one's
sense of freedom to choose and act. The modality of possibility is perhaps a depersonalized projection of the subjective sense of capability, a projection reminiscent of the
animists' projection of spirits into the rocks and trees.
Necessity, then, would be a projection of the subjective
sense of constraint, or abridgment of capability.

I suppose the idea even of efficient cause was mentalistic
in origin, being a projection of the subjective sense of effort.
Anyway it gained the upper hand over final cause with the
rise of physics in the Renaissance. Concomitantly, matter
gained the upper hand over mind. Mind was selflessly do-
ing itself in. Matter and efficient cause were a formidable
combination, vindicated in waves of successful prediction.

Final cause still had its explanatory duties too, not only in
relation to the mind of man but also in biology, where it
became an embarrassment, depriving biology of the aus-
terely scientific status that physics had come to enjoy. Dar-
win at length settled that matter, reducing final cause in
biology to efficient cause through his theory of natural
selection.

Efficient cause figures conspicuously still in fairly austere science. It is not clearly intensional, in the sense of resisting substitutivity of identity, but it is like the intensional idioms in lodging sentences indigestibly within sentences. We cannot resolve 'p because q' into predicates, quantifiers, and truth functions, nor do we have as clear a notion of cause as we could wish. Science at its more austere bypasses the notion and settles for concomitances.

Disposition is like cause in admitting substitutivity of identity but resisting the predicate calculus. Also it is like cause in its want of clarity. It seems to rest on an uncomfortable notion of potentiality. But these discomforts can be quickly dissipated, for there is no need to invest the dispositional suffixes '-ble' and '-ile' with any theoretical content. 'Fragile' and 'soluble' are physical predicates on a par with others, and the dispositional form of the words is just a laconic encoding of a relatively dependable test or symptom. Breaking on impact and dissolving on immersion are symptomatic of fragility and solubility. See *Roots of Reference,* §§3–4.

V

TRUTH

32. Vehicles of truth

What are true or false, it will be widely agreed, are propositions. But it would not be so widely agreed were it not for ambiguity of 'proposition'. Some understand the word as referring to sentences meeting certain specifications. Others understand it as referring rather to the meanings of such sentences. What looked like wide agreement thus resolves into two schools of thought: for the first school the vehicles of truth and falsity are the sentences, and for the second they are the meanings of the sentences.

A weakness of this second position is the tenuousness of the notion of sentence meanings. The tenuousness reaches the breaking point if one is pursuaded of my thesis of the indeterminacy of translation (§§18, 21). Even apart from that thesis, it seems perverse to bypass the visible or audible sentences and to center upon sentence meanings as truth vehicles; for it is only by recurring to the sentence that we can say which sentence meaning we have in mind.

There was indeed a motive for pressing to the sentence meanings. Many sentences in the same or different languages are deemed to be alike in meaning, and distinctions among them are indifferent to truth; so one narrowed the field by ascribing truth rather to the meanings. This motive would be excellent if the notion of sentence meaning were not so elusive. But as matters stand we fare better by treating directly of sentences. These we can get our teeth into.

There was also a second motive, equal and opposite to the first, for pressing on to the sentence meanings; namely, that one and the same sentence can be true on some occasions and false on others. Thus 'The Pope will visit Boston' was true but turned false after his last visit. 'I have a headache' is true or false depending on who says it and when. Ambiguity or vagueness of terms, also, can cause the truth value of a sentence to depend in part on the speaker's intention.

Propositions, thought of as sentence meanings, were the meanings exclusively of sentences of a firmer sort, not subject to such vacillations; what we may call *eternal* sentences.[1] My obvious response, then, is that those eternal sentences themselves can serve as the truth vehicles. Just think of 'I', 'you', 'he', 'she', 'here', and 'there' as supplanted by names and addresses or other identifying particulars as needed. Think of tenses as dropped; we can use dates, the predicate 'earlier than', and the like as needed. Think of ambiguities and vaguenesses as resolved by paraphrase—not absolutely, but enough to immobilize the truth value of the particular sentence. The truth values need not be known, but they must be stable.

The attitude is the one that is familiar in the teaching of logic. When we take illustrative sentences from everyday

---

[1] In my logic books of 1940, 1941, and 1950, and revised editions down the years, my word for them was 'statement'; but I became chary of it because of its customary use rather for an act. 'Eternal sentence', along with 'standing sentence' (§4), dates from *Word and Object*. 'Standing sentence' is more inclusive. 'The *Times* has come' is a standing sentence, for it can command assent all day independently of interim stimulation; but it is not eternal.

language and paraphrase them into the notation of truth functions and quantifiers, we think of the reference of demonstratives and personal pronouns as fixed—albeit tacitly—and we never dream of reading '∃x' as 'there was' or 'there will be something x'.

Declarative sentences thus refined—eternal sentences—are what I shall regard as truth vehicles in ensuing pages, for the most part. On the whole it is the convenient line for theoretical purposes. We must recognize, though, that it bypasses most of what counts in daily discourse as true or false, since our utterances are not for the most part thus refined. The truth vehicles directly related to behavior are not sentences as repeatable linguistic forms, but rather the individual acts of uttering them. These are for the most part univocal in truth value without benefit of paraphrase. There are just occasional failures, perhaps because some name turns out to be empty or because some vague term turns out to be indeterminate just where it matters for the utterance in question. Such utterances may be dismissed as neither true nor false.

So much by way of coming to terms with the realities of verbal behavior. Let us now return to the more conveniently manageable domain of eternal sentences, whose truth or falsity, known or unknown, is unchanging.

33. Truth as disquotation

Such being what admit of truth, then, wherein does their truth consist? They qualify as true, one is told, by corresponding to reality. But correspondence word by word will not do; it invites the idle cluttering of reality with a bizarre host of fancied objects, just for the sake of correspondence.

A neater plan is to posit *facts,* as correspondents of true sentences as wholes; but this still is a put-up job. Objects in abundance, concrete and abstract, are indeed needed for an account of the world; but facts contribute nothing beyond their specious support of a correspondence theory.

Yet there is some underlying validity to the correspondence theory of truth, as Tarski has taught us. Instead of saying that

> 'Snow is white' is true if and only if it is a fact that snow is white

we can simply delete 'it is a fact that' as vacuous, and therewith facts themselves:

> 'Snow is white' is true if and only if snow is white.

To ascribe truth to the sentence is to ascribe whiteness to snow; such is the correspondence, in this example. Ascription of truth just cancels the quotation marks. Truth is disquotation.

So the truth predicate is superfluous when ascribed to a given sentence; you could just utter the sentence. But it is needed for sentences that are not given. Thus we may want to say that everything someone said on some occasion was true, or that all consequences of true theories are true. Such contexts, when analyzed logically, exhibit the truth predicate in application not to a quotation but to a pronoun, or bound variable.

The truth predicate proves invaluable when we want to generalize along a dimension that cannot be swept out by a general term. The easy sort of generalization is illustrated by generalization on the term 'Socrates' in 'Socrates is mortal'; the sentence generalizes to 'All men are mortal'. The general term 'man' has served to sweep out the desired dimension of generality. The harder sort of generalization is illustrated by generalization on the clause 'time flies' in 'If time flies then time flies'. We want to say that this compound continues true when the clause is supplanted by any other; and we can do no better than to say just that in so many words, including the word 'true'. We say "All sentences of the form 'If p then p' are true." We could not generalize as in 'All men are mortal', because 'time flies' is not, like 'Socrates', a name of one of a range of objects (men) over which to generalize. We cleared this obstacle by *semantic ascent:* by ascending to a level where there were indeed objects over which to generalize, namely linguistic objects, sentences.

Semantic ascent serves also outside of logic. When Einstein propounded relativity, disrupting our basic conceptions of distance and time, it was hard to assess it without leaning on our basic conceptions and thus begging the question. But by semantic ascent one could compare the new and old theories as symbolic structures, and so appreciate that the new theory organized the pertinent data more simply than the old. Simplicity of symbolic structures can be appreciated independently of those basic conceptions.

As already hinted by the correspondence theory, the truth predicate is an intermediary between words and the world. What is true is the sentence, but its truth consists in the world's being as the sentence says. Hence the use of the truth predicate in accommodating semantic ascent.

The disquotational account of truth does not define the truth predicate—not in the strict sense of 'definition'; for definition in the strict sense tells how to eliminate the defined expression from every desired context in favor of previously established notation. But in a looser sense the disquotational account does define truth. It tells us what it is for any sentence to be true, and it tells us this in terms just as clear to us as the sentence in question itself. We understand what it is for the sentence 'Snow is white' to be true as clearly as we understand what it is for snow to be white. Evidently one who puzzles over the adjective 'true' should puzzle rather over the sentences to which he ascribes it. 'True' is transparent.

For eternal sentences the disquotational account of truth is neat, we see, and simple. It is readily extended, moreover, to the workaday world of individual utterances; thus an utterance of 'I have a headache' is true if and only if the utterer has a headache while uttering it.

34. *Paradox*

It seems paradoxical that the truth predicate, for all its transparency, should prove useful to the point of indispensability. In the matter of paradox, moreover, this is scarcely the beginning. Truth is notoriously enmeshed in paradox, to the point of out-and-out antinomy.

An ancient form of the antinomy of truth is the Paradox of the Liar: 'I am lying', or 'This sentence is not true'. A looser and fancier version was the paradox of Epimenides the Cretan, who said that all Cretans were liars. The underlying antinomy can be purified for logical purposes to read thus:

(1)   'yields a falsehood when appended to its own
        quotation' yields a falsehood when appended to
        its own quotation.

Executing the instructions in (1), we append the nine-word expression to its quotation. The result is (1) itself. Thus (1) says that (1) itself is a falsehood. It is thus tantamount to 'I am lying', but more clean-cut. It hinges only on the innocuous operations of quoting and appending and the notion of falsehood, which reduces to an innocent 'not' and *true*. The truth predicate is clearly the trouble spot. The inevitable conclusion is that the truth predicate, for all its transparency and seeming triviality, is incoherent unless somehow restricted.

For further explicitness a technical turn of phrase will be convenient. The truth predicate will be said to *disquote* a sentence S if the form

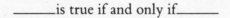

_____is true if and only if_____

comes out true when S is named in the first blank and written in the second. Thus what the disquotational account of truth says is that the truth predicate disquotes every eternal sentence. But the lesson of the antinomy is that if a language has at its disposal the innocent notations for treating of quoting and appending, and also the notations of elementary logic, then it cannot contain also a truth predicate that disquotes all its own eternal sentences—on pain of inconsistency. Its truth predicate, or its best approximation to one, must be incompletely disquotational. Specifically, it must not disquote all the sentences that contain it. That was the trouble with (1). And of course it must not disquote all the sentences containing terms by which that predicate could be paraphrased. This, apart from its special orientation to quoting and appending, is substantially what has come to be known as Tarski's Theorem. He has proved harder things.

The truth predicate loses little in general utility thereby, for it can still disquote all the eternal sentences that do not themselves contain it or other expressions to the same effect. And even these excluded applications can be accommodated by a hierarchy of truth predicates. The hierarchy begins with a predicate 'true$_0$', which disquotes all sentences that contain no truth predicate or equivalent devices. A predicate 'true$_1$', next, disquotes all sentences that contain no truth predicate or equivalent devices beyond 'true$_0$'. And so on up. It is a hierarchy of progressively more nearly perfect truth predicates. The plan dates back in a way to the early phase of Russell's theory of types (1908), by which he meant to obstruct the Paradox of the Liar among others.

35. Tarski's construction

We saw that disquotation is loosely definitive of truth. We may now be thankful for the looseness, seeing as we do that definability of truth for a language within the language would be an embarrassment. And thus it was that Tarski undertook the perilous adventure of defining it for the language within the language, as nearly as possible, if only to see what minimum obstacle saved the situation. This was not his order of presentation, but it comes out the same.

The language chosen for the construction contains the logical notations for quantification and the truth functions and the set-theoretic notation '$x \in y$' for membership.[2] It contains also a finite lexicon, as large as you please, of predicates for natural science and daily life. Finally it contains the

[2] Readers expecting a contrast between object language and metalanguage should bear in mind that I am already addressing the aforesaid perilous adventure.

means, in effect, of quoting and appending, as in (1); that is, it can specify each of its single signs and it can express the concatenation of expressions.

Truth pertains to closed sentences, that is, sentences without free variables. Its analogue for open sentences is the two-place predicate of *satisfaction*. An assignment of objects to variables *satisfies* a sentence if the sentence is true for those values of its free variables.

What sort of object is an *assignment* of objects to variables? It is simply a function, or one-many *relation*, relating one and only one object to each variable—that is, to each letter, 'w', 'x', 'y', 'z', 'w'', etc. A relation, in turn, is a set, or class, or *ordered pairs*. Ways are well known of defining the notation '$\langle x, y \rangle$' of ordered pairs contextually by means of epsilon and the logical particles.

Once satisfaction is defined, truth comes easily; for a closed sentence, having no free variables, is vacuously satisfied by all assignments or none according as it is true or false. We can simply define

(2)   'y is true' as '$\forall x(x$ is assignment $\cdot \rightarrow \cdot x$ satisfies $y)$'.

So Tarski's big job is to define satisfaction. First he defines it for *atomic* sentences, each of which consists of just a predicate adjoined to one or more variables. For instance an assignment satisfies the atomic sentence '$x \in y$' if and only if what is assigned to the letter 'x' is a member of what is assigned to the letter 'y'. Correspondingly for each of the other predicates in the lexicon. An assignment satisfies an alternation of sentences, next, if and only if it satisfies one or both of them; it satisfies their conjunction if and only if it satisfies both; and it satisfies a negation if and only if it does not satisfy the sentence that is negated. Finally, an assignment satisfies an existential quantification '$\exists x(\ldots x \ldots)$' if and only if some assignment, matching that one except perhaps for what it assigns to 'x', satisfies '$\ldots x \ldots$'.

Such is Tarski's recursive or inductive definition of satisfaction. It explains satisfaction of atomic sentences outright, and it explains satisfaction of sentences of each higher grade or complexity in terms of satisfaction of their components. Universal quantification is passed over because it is expressible in terms of existential quantification and negation in familiar fashion.

36. Paradox skirted

Clearly all the clauses of this inductive definition can be formulated within the formal language itself, except for the word 'satisfies' that is being defined. Thus we have apparantly defined satisfaction for the language within the language. Invoking (2), then, we have done the same for truth. This was supposed to spell contradiction.

We could even get contradiction directly from satisfaction, without the detour through (2), 'truth', and (1). We have merely to ask whether assignment of the sentence 'not (x satisfies x)' to the variable 'x' satisfies the sentence 'not (x satisfies x)' itself. Such is Grelling's so-called Heterological Paradox.[3]

What saves the situation is that the definition of satisfaction is inductive rather than direct. The inductive definition explains satisfaction of each specific sentence, but it does not provide a translation of 'x satisfies y' with variable 'y'.

[3] See my Ways of Paradox, pp. 4–6.

Consequently it does not translate the 'not (x satisfies x)' of Grelling's paradox, and does not support the truth definition (2) for variable 'γ'; it just explains truth of each specific closed sentence. It leaves the truth predicate in the same state in which the disquotational account left it; namely, fully explained in application to each specific sentence of the given language but not in application to a variable.

It was a near miss, and I turn now to a nearer one. Treating relations again as classes of ordered pairs, we can write '$\langle x,y \rangle \in z$' to mean that x bears the relation z to y. Now imagine the above inductive definition of satisfaction written out in our formal language, with the variable 'z' always in place of 'satisfies' and so '$\langle x, y \rangle \in z$' in place of '$x$ satisfies y'. Let the whole inductive definition, thus edited, be abbreviated as 'Φz'. It fixes z as the satisfaction relation. Evidently we arrive thus at a *direct* definition:

(3) $\exists z(\Phi z \cdot \langle x, y \rangle \in z)$

of 'x satisfies y' strictly within the formal language itself. Doesn't this spell contradiction?

No. The catch this time is that there might not be any relation z such that Φz. Indeed there better not be, on pain, we see, of contradiction. The two-place predicate 'satisfies' remains well defined in its inductive way, but a grasp of the predicate and how to use it carries no assurance of the existence of a corresponding abstract object, a corresponding set of ordered pairs. And, failing such a pair set, (3) fails to translate 'x satisfies y'. Though the satisfaction predicate is well explained even within the formal language by the recursion, it does not get reduced to the prior notation of that language. Satisfaction, and truth along with it, retain the status that truth already enjoyed under the disquotation account: clear intelligibility without full eliminability.[4]

37. *Interlocked hierarchies*

The inductive definition fully explains what it is for an assignment to satisfy a sentence. That there is such a satisfaction relation, then, or pair set, is sheer common sense. The paradoxes of set theory, however—Russell's, Burali-Forti's, Cantor's—have overruled the commonsense notion that clear membership conditions assure the existence of a class, a set. All of those were paradoxes ultimately of the membership predicate 'ε'; what is striking about the present case is just that we find set theory responding also to paradoxes of truth and satisfaction.

Some mathematicians supplement the universe of classes, or sets, with a layer of classes that are not eligible for membership in any further classes. The hitherto interchangeable terms 'set' and 'class' are then used to mark the distinction: sets are classes that *are* members of further classes. The added classes, members of nothing, came to be known lamely as classes *proper*, or "proper classes." I have called them *ultimate* classes. Membership conditions that failed to determine sets can be reinstated without fear of contradiction as determining ultimate classes. Luxuriously, thenceforward, every membership condition on sets determines a class; maybe it will be a set, maybe an ultimate class. Parsons has shown (pp. 212–214) that the satisfaction rela-

[4] The foregoing analysis is adapted from my *Philosophy of Logic*, pp. 35–46. A somewhat different analysis, in my 1952 paper "On an Application of Tarski's Theory of Truth," is called for when the set theory is of the kind that admits both sets and ultimate classes.

tion that had failed to exist as a set of pairs now comes to exist as an ultimate class of pairs. A direct definition of satisfaction, and so of truth, is thus achieved after all. But it is achieved only for sentences of the old theory, unsupplemented with ultimate classes.

Thus let us suppose that along with adding the ultimate classes we introduced a new style of variables, to range over classes generally—the old variables being limited to sets. Then the point is that truth, as newly and directly defined, is assured of disquotationality over all the old sentences, but will fail of it for some sentences containing the new variables.

But we can repeat the expedient, adding layer on layer of new classes without end. 'Ultimate' ceases to be the word now; I must submit to 'proper class'. The classes at each level admit members freely from all and only lower levels. For the ith level, for each i, the variables 'x_i', 'y_i', etc. range over that level and lower ones; thus 'x_0', 'y_0', etc. range only over sets. Predicates 'true$_0$', 'true$_1$', and so on are then all forthcoming by direct definition. For each i, 'true$_i$' is dependably disquotational in application to sentences containing no bound variables beyond level i. We get a self-contained language with a hierarchy of better and better truth predicates but no best. Truth$_0$ is already good enough for most purposes, including classical mathematics.

In his early version of his theory of types, mentioned at the end of §34, Russell sought to block the paradoxes both of truth and of membership by decreeing a single complex hierarchy of predicates. The scheme was vague and cumbersome. He and others subsequently sharpened and simplified it for purposes of set theory by dispensing with the truth aspect as extraneous to set theory. And now we see a new interlocking of the class hierarchy with the truth hierarchy, along clean-cut lines and for clear but subtle reasons that could not be foreseen in Russell's day.

I have pictured the hierarchy of class variables and the hierarchy of truth predicates as embraced within a single inclusive language. This is how I like it. But alternatively we can picture a hierarchy of languages, each with single-sorted variables and a unique truth predicate for the next lower language. This approach has an important mathematical application in establishing relative strengths of formal systems. To prove that one system is stronger than another, reinterpret its predicates in such a way as to be able to define, within it, the truth predicate of the other system.

38. *Excluded middle*

Let us look into some seemingly deviant notions about truth. One such, traceable to Aristotle, is that a prediction is neither true nor false until events have occurred that causally determine it. Theologians have favored the doctrine. If contingent predictions were true now, they reason, the events would be determined now by God's knowledge, and hence would not be contingent. The consequent determinism, it is felt, would leave no place for man's moral responsibility.

This doctrine, for all its bizarreness, is no repudiation of the disquotational account of truth. If it is not yet *true* that there will be a sea-fight tomorrow—to take Aristotle's example—then it is a mistake to say now that there will *be* a sea-fight tomorrow; for as of now the contingent sentence is neither true nor false. The logic, granted, is deviant: the law of excluded middle is suspended pending causal determination. But the disquotational character of truth remains.

Bizarreness remains too. There is the abandonment of the law of excluded middle; also the drastic narrowing of the range of sentences with fixed truth values. Happily, however, the theological argument underlying this desperate move is inconclusive on two points. One is the assumption of an omniscient God. The other is the notion that universal determinism precludes freedom of action. We are free and responsible, it can be argued, in that we act as we choose to; whether our choices are determined by prior causes is beside the point.

Some other apparent challenges to the law of excluded middle are, in part, not what they seem. Let it be clear, to begin with, that ignorance of the truth or falsity of a sentence is par for the course, and quite in keeping with its being true or false. Further, it commonly happens that a sentence can be rendered eternal in divergent ways, reflecting a speaker's intentions in different situations. Here it is rather the respective utterances that are true or false, together with their full unambiguous elaborations if we care to elaborate them. The original ambiguous sentence is indeed then neither true nor false, but this need not be seen as a breach of the law of excluded middle; it is better seen as an incompleteness that has still to be filled out in one or another way. This line was not available in the case of the theologians' strictures on contingent predictions, because those sentences were meant still to become true or false, without supplementation, once they stopped being contingent.

There is another and stronger case that likewise threatens the law of excluded middle. It is where a purported name or singluar description fails to designate anything. When a sentence contains such a term, one possible line is to drop the sentence from consideration; treat it as meaningless. This line is awkward when we regiment our sentences for logical purposes, for the existence of the object may be an open question—as in the case of Camelot or Prester John or the outermost satellite of Pluto. It is quite in order for the truth value of a sentence to remain an open question, but it is inconvenient to leave the very meaningfulness of a sentence forever unsettled.

One might accordingly relinquish the law of excluded middle and opt rather for a three-valued logic, recognizing a limbo between truth and falsity as a third truth value. What then comes to hinge on existence of Camelot, or whatever, is truth value rather than meaningfulness, and that is as it should be. But a price is paid in the cumbersomeness of three-valued logic. Alongside 'not', which sends truths into falsehoods, falsehoods into truths, and now limbo into limbo, there would be a truth function that sends truths into limbo, limbo into falsehoods, and falsehoods into truths; also three more such one-place truth functions, playing out the combinations—as contrasted with a single one, negation, in two-valued logic. When we move out to two-place truth functions (conjunction, alternation, and their derivatives), proliferation runs amok. It can still be handled, but there is an evident premium on our simple streamlined two-valued logic.

We can adhere to the latter, in the face anyway of the threat of empty singular terms, by simply dispensing with singular terms as in §10. 'Camelot is fair' becomes '$\exists x(x$ is Camelot and x is fair)'. It does not go into limbo; it simply goes false if it is false that $\exists x(x$ is Camelot). The predicate 'is Camelot' is seen on a par with 'is fair', as a predicate irreducibly.

39. *Truth versus warranted belief*

Pilate was probably not the first to ask what truth is, and he was by no means the last. Those who ask it seek something deeper than disquotation, which was the valid residue of the correspondence theory of truth (§33). Yet there is surely no impugning the disquotation account; no disputing that 'Snow is white' is true if and only if snow is white. Moreover, it is a full account: it explicates clearly the truth or falsity of every clear sentence. It is even a more than full account: it imposes a requirement on the truth predicate that is too strong for any predicate within the language concerned—on pain of contradiction (§34).

There are recurrent references to a coherence theory of truth, or a pragmatist theory of truth. The question that motivates this quest beyond disquotation can perhaps be phrased thus: if to call a sentence true is simply to affirm it, then how can we tell whether to affirm it?

The lazy answer is "That all depends on what the sentence is. In the case of 'Snow is white' you just look at snow and check the color." The more sympathetic answer is a general analysis of the grounds of warranted belief, hence scientific method—perhaps along the lines of §§2–7.

The moderately holistic considerations there set forth are uncongenial to a line currently urged by Michael Dummett, in which he contests the law of excluded middle on epistemological grounds. The attack was mounted in mathematics by L. E. J. Brouwer early in this century, and Dummett adopts the attitude toward science in general. His rough idea is to reckon a sentence of natural science neither true nor false if no procedure is known for making a strong empirical case for its truth or falsity.

Holistic considerations make it doubtful what sentences should be retained, then, as eligible for truth or falsity. Clear candidates for retention are the observation categoricals. Other sentences share empirical content in varying degrees by implying observation categoricals jointly. It seems vain to seek an invidious distinction between sentences eligible for truth or falsity and sentences in limbo, unless we either draw that boundary at the observation categoricals themselves or else draw it at the far extreme to exclude just those sentences that never imbibe any empirical content by participating in the joint implying of any observation categoricals.

Truth is one thing, warranted belief another. We can gain clarity and enjoy the sweet simplicity of two-valued logic by heeding the distinction.

40. *Truth in mathematics*

What now of those parts of mathematics that share no empirical meaning, because of never getting applied in natural science? What of the higher reaches of set theory? We see them as meaningful because they are couched in the same grammar and vocabulary that generate the applied parts of mathematics. We are just sparing ourselves the unnatural gerrymandering of grammar that would be needed to exclude them. On our two-valued approach they then qualify as true or false, albeit inscrutably.

They are not wholly inscrutable. The main axioms of set theory are generalities operative already in the applicable part of the domain. Further sentences such as the continuum hypothesis and the axiom of choice, which are independent of those axioms, can still be submitted to the considerations of simplicity, economy, and naturalness that contribute to the molding of scientific theories generally. Such considerations support Gödel's axiom of constructibility, 'V = L'.[5] It inactivates the more gratuitous flights of higher set theory, and incidentally it implies the axiom of choice and the continuum hypothesis. More sweeping economies have been envisioned by Hermann Weyl, Paul Lorenzen, Errett Bishop, and currently Hao Wang and Solomon Feferman, who would establish that all the mathematical needs of science can be supplied on the meager basis of what has come to be known as predicative set theory.[6] Such gains are of a piece with the simplifications and economies that are hailed as progress within natural science itself. It is a matter of tightening and streamlining our global system of the world.

41. *Equivalent theories*

I defined empirical content in §7 only for testable theories, and I went on to point out that much solid experimental science fails of testability in the defined sense. This can happen, we saw, because of vague and uncalibrated probabilities in the backlog of theory. No doubt it happens also in more complex ways, not clearly understood. I have no definition of empirical content to offer for such theories, but it still seems to make reasonable intuitive sense to speak of empirical equivalence among them, since experimenta-

[5] See my *Set Theory and Its Logic*, 2d ed., pp. 234–238.

[6] See *Quiddities*, pp. 34–36.

tion is still brought to bear. The idea is that whatever observation would be counted for or against the one theory counts equally for or against the other. What I shall have to say about empirically equivalent theories applies indifferently to testable ones and to theories that are empirically equivalent in this ill-defined way.

Theories can differ utterly in their objects, over which their variables of quantification range, and still be empirically equivalent, as proxy functions show (§12). We hardly seem warranted in calling them two theories; they are two ways of expressing one and the same theory. It is interesting, then, that a theory can thus vary its ontology.

Effort and paper have been wasted, by me among others, over what to count as sameness of theory and what to count as mere equivalence. It is a question of words; we can stop speaking of theories and just speak of theory formulations. I shall still write simply 'theory', but you may understand it as 'theory formulation' if you will.

Theories (theory formulations) can be logically incompatible and still be empirically equivalent. A familiar example is Riemannian and Euclidean geometry as applied to the surface of a sphere. Riemannian geometry says that straight lines always meet. Euclidean geometry says that some do and some do not, and in particular that there are none on a sphere. The conflict is resolved by reinterpreting 'straight line' in the Riemannian glossary as 'great circle'.

The next example, due to Poincaré (ch. 4), is less trivial. We have on the one hand our commonsense conception of infinite space and rigid bodies that move freely without shrinking or stretching, and on the other hand the conception of a finite spherical space in which those bodies shrink uniformly as they move away from center. Both conceptions can be reconciled with all possible observations; they are empirically equivalent. Yet they differ, this time, more deeply than in the mere choice of words. The theory with the finite space makes crucial use of a theoretical term that admits of no counterpart in the theory with the infinite space—namely, 'center of space'.

Imagine now two theories, ours and another, such that we are persuaded of their empirical equivalence but we see no way of systematically converting one into the other by reinterpretation sentence by sentence, as we did in the example of the proxy function and that of the sphere. There are three cases to consider.

Case 1: The other theory is logically compatible with our own and is expressed directly in our own terms. It differs from ours in that it implies some theoretical sentences that ours leaves unsettled, and vice versa. Yet the theories are empirically equivalent. This case presents no problem. We would simply accept the other theory and incorporate it into our own as an enrichment, answering many theoretical questions that ours left open.

Case 2: Again the other theory is logically compatible with ours, but, like Poincaré's example, it hinges on some theoretical terms not reducible to ours.

Case 3: The two theories are logically incompatible. Donald Davidson showed me that this case can be reduced to Case 2 by the following maneuver. Take any sentence S that the one theory implies and the other denies. Since the theories are empirically equivalent, S must hinge on some theoretical term that is not firmly pinned down to observable criteria. We may then exploit its empirical slack by treating that term as two terms, distinctively spelled in the two theories. S thus gives way to two mutually independent sentences S and S'. Continuing thus, we can make the two theories logically compatible.

42. Irresoluble rivalry

So we may limit our attention to Case 2. Let us limit it further to global systems of the world, so that there is no question of fitting the rival theories into a broader context. So we are imagining a global system empirically equivalent to our own and logically compatible with ours but hinging on alien terms. It may seem that as staunch empiricists we should reckon both theories as true. Still, this line is unattractive if the other theory is less simple and natural than ours; and indeed there is no limit to how grotesquely cumbersome a theory might be and still be empirically equivalent to an elegant one. We do better, in such a case, to take advantage of the presence of irreducibly alien terms. We can simply bar them from our language as meaningless. After all, they are not adding to what our own theory can predict, any more than 'phlogiston' or 'entelechy' does, or indeed 'fate', 'grace', 'nirvana', 'mana'. We thus consign all contexts of the alien terms to the limbo of nonsentences.

We have here an encroachment of coherence considerations upon standards of truth. Simplicity and naturalness are making the difference between truth and meaninglessness.

We might still choose to enrich our original theory with any novel findings of the other theory that do not use the alien terms. It would be a matter of welcoming information from a presumed dependable outside source, much as supplementary truths of number theory are got by excursions through analysis, or as the four-color-map question was settled by an elaborate computer program.

But now suppose rather that the rival theory is as neat and natural as our own. Our empiricist scruples reawaken. Should we incorporate that theory into our own, as in Case 1? No, this would ill accord with the scientists' quest for simplicity and economy; for the irreducible new terms imported with the annexed theory have added no new coverage of observables. The two theories were already empirically equivalent to each other, and hence to their conjunction. The two theories were streamlined and neck-and-neck, but the tandem theory is loaded beyond necessity: loaded with all the sentences containing the new terms.

One possible attitude to adopt toward the two theories is a *sectarian* one, as I have called it: [7] treat the rival theory as in the preceding case, by rejecting all the contexts of its alien terms. We can no longer excuse this unequal treatment of the two theories on the ground that our own is more elegant, but still we can plead that we have no higher access to truth than our evolving theory, however fallible. Dagfinn Føllesdal and Roger Gibson abetted me in this sectarian attitude. The opposing attitude is the *ecumenical* one, which would count both theories true. Its appeal is empiricism: reluctance to discriminate invidiously between empirically equivalent and equally economical theories. The tandem theory, which we found prohibitively uneconomical, was one ecumenical line. But a different ecumenical line has been urged by Donald Davidson: that we account both theories separately true, the truth predicate being under-

[7] "Reply to Gibson."

stood now as disquotation in an inclusive and theory-neutral language in which both theories are couched. In recent years I have vacillated among these alternatives, which are now down to two: the sectarian line and the ecumenical line à la Davidson.

The latter alternative raises questions regarding the inclusive language. It would include all terms of both of the rival systems of the world, and its variables would range over both ontologies. Distinctive predicates would serve to delimit values of the variables to the one ontology or the other as needed. How much more widely should the variables range? And what of truth: will there be a hierarchy of truth predicates and a matching hierarchy of styles of variables, as at the end of §37? We must call a halt. We sought only an inclusive language, not a third theory.

What is to be gained is not evident, apart from the satisfaction of conferring the cachet of truth evenhandedly. The sectarian is no less capable than the ecumenist of appreciating the equal evidential claims of the two rival theories of the world. He can still be evenhanded with the cachet of warrantedness, if not of truth. Moreover he is as free as the ecumenist to oscillate between the two theories for the sake of added perspective from which to triangulate on problems. In his sectarian way he does deem the one theory true and the alien terms of the other theory meaningless, but only so long as he is entertaining the one theory rather than the other. He can readily shift the shoe to the other foot.

The fantasy of irresolubly rival systems of the world is a thought experiment out beyond where linguistic usage has been crystallized by use. No wonder the cosmic question whether to call two such world systems true should simmer down, bathetically, to a question of words. Hence also, meanwhile, my vacillation.

Fare these conventions as they may, the rival theories describe one and the same world. Limited to our human terms and devices, we grasp the world variously. I think of the disparate ways of getting at the diameter of an impenetrable sphere: we may pinion the sphere in calipers or we may girdle it with a tape measure and divide by pi, but there is no getting inside.

43. *Two indeterminacies*

There is an evident parallel between the empirical underdetermination of global science and the indeterminacy of translation. In both cases the totality of possible evidence is insufficient to clinch the system uniquely. But the indeterminacy of translation is additional to the other. If we settle upon one of the empirically equivalent systems of the world, however arbitrarily, we still have within it the indeterminacy of translation.

Another distinctive point about the indeterminacy of translation is that it clearly has nothing to do with inaccessible facts and human limitations. Dispositions to observable behavior are all there is for semantics to be right or wrong about (§14). In the case of systems of the world, on the other hand, one is prepared to believe that reality exceeds the scope of the human apparatus in unspecifiable ways.

Let us now look more closely to parallels. On the one hand we have the two incompatible but equally faithful systems of translation; each propounds some translations that the other rejects. On the other hand we have two incompatible but empirically equivalent systems of the world. We noted in §18 that we can reconcile the two systems of translation by recognizing them as defining different relations, translation$_1$ and translation$_2$. We noted in §41 that we can reconcile the two systems of the world by similarly splitting one or more theoretical terms.

What the indeterminacy of translation shows is that the notion of propositions as sentence meanings is untenable. What the empirical under-determination of global science shows is that there are various defensible ways of conceiving the world.

REFERENCES

CREDITS

INDEX

REFERENCES

Barrett, R. B., and R. F. Gibson, eds. *Perspectives on Quine*. Oxford: Blackwell. In press.

Bergström, Lars. "Quine on Underdetermination." In Barrett and Gibson.

Carnap, Rudolf. *Logische Syntax der Sprache*. Vienna, 1934.

Chisholm, Roderick. *Perceiving: A Philosophical Study*. Ithaca: Cornell University Press, 1957.

Davidson, Donald. *Essays on Action and Events*. Oxford: Clarendon, 1980.

Dennett, Daniel. *The Intentional Stance*. Cambridge: MIT Press, 1987.

Duhem, Pierre. *La théorie physique: son objet et sa structure*. Paris, 1906.

Dummett, Michael. *Truth and Other Enigmas*. Cambridge: Harvard University Press, 1978.

Firth, Roderick. "Reply to Sellars." *Monist* 64 (1981), pp. 91–101.

Grünbaum, Adolf. "The Falsifiability of Theories." *Synthese* 14 (1962), pp. 17–34.

Kirk, Robert. "Quine's Indeterminacy Thesis." *Mind* 78 (1969), pp. 607–608.

Levy, Edwin. "Competing Radical Translations." *Boston Studies in Philosophy of Science* 8 (1971), pp. 590–605.

Lewis, C. I. *An Analysis of Knowledge and Valuation*. La Salle: Open Court, 1946.

Massey, G. J. "Indeterminacy, Inscrutability, and Ontological Relativity." *American Philosophical Quarterly*, Monograph 12 (1978), pp. 43–55.

Parsons, Charles. *Mathematics and Philosophy*. Ithaca: Cornell University Press, 1983.

Poincaré, Henri. *Science and Hypothesis*. New York, 1905.

Popper, Sir Karl. *The Logic of Scientific Discovery*. New York: Basic Books, 1959.

Premack, David. *Gavagai*. Cambridge: MIT Press, 1986.

Putnam, Hilary. "Mathematics without Foundations." *Journal of Philosophy* 64 (1967), pp. 5–22.

Quine, W. V. *Mathematical Logic*. New York, 1940. Corrected ed. (thanks to Wang), Cambridge: Harvard University Press, 1951.

——— *Elementary Logic*. Boston, 1941. Rev. ed., Harvard University Press, 1965.

——— *Methods of Logic*. New York, 1950. 3d ed., 1972. 4th, Harvard University Press, 1982.

——— "On an Application of Tarski's Theory of Truth." *Proceedings of the National Academy of Sciences* 38 (1952), pp. 430–433. Rpt. in *Selected Logic Papers*. New York: Random House, 1966.

——— *From a Logical Point of View*. Harvard University Press, 1953.

——— *Word and Object*. Cambridge: MIT Press, 1960.

——— *Set Theory and Its Logic*. Harvard University Press, 1963. Rev. ed., 1969.

——— *The Ways of Paradox and Other Essays*. New York, 1966. Enlarged ed., Harvard University Press, 1976.

——— *Ontological Relativity and Other Essays*. New York: Columbia University Press, 1969.

——— *Philosophy of Logic*. Englewood Cliffs, N.J., 1970; Harvard University Press, 1986.

——— *Roots of Reference*, La Salle: Open Court, 1974.

——— "The Nature of Natural Knowledge." In J. Guttenplan, ed. *Mind and Language* (Oxford: Clarendon Press, 1975), pp. 67–81.

——— *Theories and Things*. Harvard University Press, 1981.

——— "Events and Reification." In E. Lepore and B. McLaughlin, eds., *Action and Events* (Oxford: Blackwell, 1985), pp. 162–171.

——— "Reply to Roger F. Gibson, Jr." In L. E. Hahn and P. A. Schilpp, eds., *The Philosophy of W. V. Quine* (LaSalle: Open Court, 1986), pp. 155–157.

——— *Quiddities*. Harvard University Press, 1987.

Quine, W. V., and J. S. Ullian. *The Web of Belief*. New York: Random House, 1970. Rev. ed., 1978.

Russell, Bertrand. "On Denoting." *Mind* 14 (1905), pp. 479–493.

——— "Mathematical Logic as Based on the Theory of Types." *American Journal of Mathematics* 30 (1908), pp. 222–262.

Sleigh, R. C. "On a Proposed System of Epistemic Logic," *Noûs* 2 (1968), pp. 391–398.

Tarski, Alfred. "The Concept of Truth in Formalized Languages." In his *Logic, Semantics, Metamathematics* (Oxford: Clarendon Press, 1956), pp. 152–278. Translated from the German of 1936.

Ullian, J. S. *See* Quine and Ullian.

Yosida, Natuhiko. "Scientific Laws and Tools for Taxonomy." *Annals of the Japanese Association for the Philosophy of Science* 6 (1984), pp. 207–218.

CREDITS

Five and a half pages are from the *Journal of Philosophy*, 1983–1987, as follows. Part of pp. 499–500 of "Ontology and Ideology Revisited" (vol. 80) appears in §10; part of p. 6 of "States of Mind" (vol. 82) appears in §24; and parts of pp. 5–9 of "Indeterminacy of Translation Again" (vol. 84) appear in §§14, 17, 18, and 23. Two pages from pp. 139–141 of "Cognitive Meaning" in the *Monist*, vol. 62, 1979, appear in §24. Most of page 164 of my reply to dalla Chiara and Toraldo di Francia in *Análisis filosófico*, vol. 2 (Buenos Aires, 1982) appears in §13. Most of p. 51 of "Sensory Support of Science," in *Discursos de investidura "Doctor Honoris Causa"*, Granada, Spain, 1986, appears in §11. I am grateful to all the copyright holders for their permission.

INDEX